Revolutions, 1789–1917

Allan Todd

Lecturer in Modern History
Workers' Educational Association,
Eastern District

CAMBRIDGE
UNIVERSITY PRESS

CAMBRIDGE UNIVERSITY PRESS
Cambridge, New York, Melbourne, Madrid, Cape Town, Singapore,
São Paulo, Delhi, Dubai, Tokyo

Cambridge University Press
The Edinburgh Building, Cambridge CB2 8RU, UK

www.cambridge.org
Information on this title: www.cambridge.org/9780521586009

First published 1998
8th printing 2006

A catalogue record for this publication is available from the British Library

ISBN 978-0-521-58600-9 Paperback

Text design by Newton Harris Design Partnership

ACKNOWLEDGEMENTS
Cover, e.t. archive; 9, 81, Giraudon/Bridgeman Art Library; 37, e.t. archive;
67, 120, David King Collection; 107, Hulton Deutsch Collection.

The cover painting, by Jacques-Louis David, shows the French revolutionary
leader, Jean-Paul Marat, dying in his bath after being stabbed by Charlotte
Corday, a Girondin supporter, on 13 July 1793.

Transferred to digital printing 2009

Contents

1 **What is revolution?**   **1**

Introduction   1
What a revolution is not   1
Revolution   2
Types of revolution   3
Revolutionary stages   5
Overview   6

2 **The old order undermined: social and economic developments**   **7**

Introduction   7
The French Revolution, 1789   7
The 1848 revolutions   11
The Paris Commune, 1871   13
The Russian Revolution, 1917   15
Document case study   *18*

3 **Political crises and revolution**   **20**

Introduction   20
The French Revolution, 1789   21
The 1848 revolutions   23
The Paris Commune, 1871   26
The Russian Revolution, 1917   28

4 **The role of ideology**   **31**

Introduction   31
The French Revolution, 1789   32
The 1848 revolutions   34
The Paris Commune, 1871   38
The Russian Revolution, 1917   39
Document case study   *42*

5 **Crowds, parties and leaders**   **45**

Introduction   45
The French Revolution, 1789   46
The 1848 revolutions   50

Contents

The Paris Commune, 1871   52
The Russian Revolution, 1917   54

6 **Barricades and blood: violence in revolutions**   **58**

Introduction   58
The French Revolution, 1789   59
The 1848 revolutions   61
The Paris Commune, 1871   63
The Russian Revolution, 1917   64
Document case study   *68*

7 **Internationalism: revolutions across borders**   **71**

Introduction   71
The French Revolution, 1789   72
The 1848 revolutions   74
The Paris Commune, 1871   76
The Russian Revolution, 1917   77

8 **Revolutionary women**   **80**

Introduction   80
The French Revolution, 1789   81
The 1848 revolutions   85
The Paris Commune, 1871   88
The Russian Revolution, 1917   90
Document case study   *93*

9 **Reaction and counter-revolution**   **99**

Introduction   99
The French Revolution, 1789   100
The 1848 revolutions   103
The Paris Commune, 1871   106
The Russian Revolution, 1917   107

10 **Revolutionary continuity: victory and defeat**   **111**

Introduction   111
The French Revolution, 1789   111
The 1848 revolutions   114
The Paris Commune, 1871   117
The Russian Revolution, 1917   118
Document case study   *122*

Select bibliography   128
Chronologies   130
Index   137

What is revolution?

Introduction

The period 1789–1917 saw four great upheavals which, either directly or indirectly, had a huge impact on the lives of millions of people. Since then, in virtually every decade and continent, the twentieth century has experienced an almost continuous cycle of revolutionary advances and counter-revolutionary setbacks. These events have generated admiration and support, or horror and opposition, depending on the aims of the revolutionaries and the beliefs of the audiences.

However, precisely because revolutions are such 'exciting times', the actual term 'revolution' is almost impossible to define in a way that would be acceptable to everyone. The very terms 'revolution' and 'revolutionary' are ones of pride or of abuse, depending on people's different political perspectives.

It is this fear and hatred of revolution that sometimes leads countries to deny much, or all, of their own revolutionary pasts. Yet, in addition to the countries to be examined in this book, there are very few states today which are not the product of revolutionary upheavals. Even Britain and the United States of America – the latter probably the most anti-revolutionary state in existence – had their own, earlier, revolutions: in the seventeenth and eighteenth centuries, respectively.

Even more confusing is the fact that the word is often used to describe *any* change in a whole range of areas: a fashion revolution, the communications revolution, or a technological revolution, for instance. Consequently, it is often easier to arrive at an understanding of revolution in a negative way, by establishing what it is not.

What a revolution is not

Not all political change and upheaval is a revolution: in fact, the majority of political struggles occurring throughout history have not been revolutions. The most common non-revolutionary forms are listed below.

- *Coup d'état / Putsch*. This is essentially the seizure of power by a relatively small group of people, often involving sections of the military. In the main, the aim of such events is to replace one group of rulers with another – the fundamental social and economic features of society are left intact.

- *Civil war*. Similar to a coup, this often starts as a political struggle for power between different groups of people who want to rule. The struggles become so intense that they spill over into the bitter violence of civil war. In the past, such disputes were common amongst royal families and those related to them; nowadays, they are frequently linked to religious or ethnic differences. But, as with coups, the leaders' main aims are usually to change a set of political rulers in order to secure power and privileges for themselves.
- *Revolt/Rebellion*. Though these can be large-scale and violent, they are not normally revolutionary. At the most, they are massive social upheavals which aim to secure a few specific reforms to improve situations which have become unacceptable. Most frequently, however, they are mass protests, organised in opposition to a particular government and some of its laws. Very often, the rebels claim to be attempting to force a return to a time when life was better; this is a feature particularly associated with the numerous peasant revolts which have erupted throughout history.

Though these political phenomena are not revolutions, each one of them can help precipitate a revolution. Coups and civil wars sometimes generate political weaknesses, and thus create opportunities for revolutionaries, while a large-scale revolt, if prolonged enough, can begin to generate increasingly radical demands and actions.

Revolution

Essentially, a revolution is when people attempt to completely transform the social, economic, political and ideological features of their society. Unlike reform or revolt, it is no longer a question of simply passing or repealing some specific laws in order to make an improvement or right a wrong. Revolution happens when enough people come to see the status quo as essentially rotten and unreformable, so that the only remedy is to sweep it all away, and to put something totally new in its place.

Contrary to popular understanding, revolution – as opposed to revolt – tends to occur when situations are beginning to improve, rather than when poverty and oppression are becoming ever more severe. This is precisely why revolutionaries are the most determined fighters for reforms – much more so than reformists, whose objectives do not go beyond achieving those reforms. This is because revolutionaries realise that poor or deteriorating conditions produce demoralisation and apathy amongst the masses. Not only does this undermine the chances of revolutionary mass actions, it even prepares the way for reaction and counter-revolution, by further weakening the mass movement. If poverty and oppression were sufficient recipes for revolution, then the whole of human history would be one of almost continuous revolution.

This desire for a new society, for fundamental change and transformation, *and* the belief that these things are now possible, help explain why revolution is a phenomenon especially associated with the young. Hope and idealism tend to be more a feature of youth than of age, so it is not surprising that young people –

especially those who continue their education – are attracted to revolutionary movements in large numbers, and are often the most ready to risk their lives. This is partly a reflection of the fact that, traditionally, societies tend to ignore and exclude young people. While conventional politicians tend to be middle-aged, or older, revolutions frequently produce young leaders who, a few years before, were virtually unknown.

For the same reasons, other marginalised sections of society – women and the poor – also tend to come to the fore in revolutionary periods. The more prolonged and deep-going the revolution, the more such groups begin to take independent action, in addition to giving their support to more general initiatives. This is why total revolution has been described as a 'festival of the oppressed': the belief that positive change is both possible and imminent is a truly intoxicating and revolutionary thought. This is one reason why counter-revolution is often so bloody – it is not just a question of prevention, revenge and punishment, but also a determination to crush the possibility of such hope for decades to come.

However, in addition to the belief in the possibility of transforming society, revolution is also linked to evolution. No revolution is a one-moment event that comes totally unexpectedly, and with no links to the preceding decades. For there to be hope that change is possible, there have to be *economic* and *social* developments that can provide a basis for such hope. Prior to successful revolutions, the old societies will have seen the appearance of new technologies, social groups and ideological developments which increasingly call into question traditional economic structures, political institutions and ways of thinking. These developments result in ever-sharper contradictions in the economic, social and political structures of existing society. In fact, without such developments, attempts at revolution will be premature and doomed to failure – either immediately or at some point in the future. For instance, many would cite the Russian Revolution of 1917, and the final collapse of the Soviet Union in 1991, as just such a case.

Types of revolution

Revolutions have various features in common. In addition to those mentioned in the previous section, *all* revolutions (as opposed to most coups, for instance) involve mass mobilisations, sometimes led by revolutionary leaders and parties, and sometimes erupting independently of the conscious wishes and intentions of such leaders and parties. While a coup, organised by a few individuals, can seize political control, revolutionaries – no matter how pure and determined – cannot transform a society without the active support and involvement of huge sections of the population.

All revolutions almost always involve a certain amount of violence. This varies according to the relative strength and determination of revolutionaries and dominant groups alike. In fact, most people's image of revolution is no doubt one of crowd violence and organised terror – most likely coloured by stories of the guillotine and Jacobin terror during the 1792–94 upheavals of the French Revolution, or by the operations of the Bolsheviks' Cheka during the civil war between Reds and Whites from 1918 to 1920. Yet, generally, it is counter-revolution rather than revolution which is more violent.

In part, the amount of mass mobilisation and violence will depend on exactly what kind of revolution is taking place. The two main types are political revolutions and social revolutions.

Political revolutions

These occur mainly when new economic and social developments have already begun to transform society, but where existing political rulers and institutions are tending to hold back further changes. The belief behind such political revolutions is that once changes in political personnel and structures have been achieved, the economic and social transformations can continue at a quicker pace, and even be assisted to their final conclusion.

The significant feature of political revolutions is that there is no intention to bring about a major transference of wealth and property from one social group to another. Very often, in fact, those pushing most strongly for a political revolution already have significant economic power – all they desire is the removal of restrictions and the provision of assistance that will enable their wealth to increase. As a consequence, political revolutions tend to be relatively bloodless. In their beginnings at least, it is possible to argue that the French Revolution of 1789 and the 1848 revolutions were both essentially political revolutions.

Social revolutions

These are much more fundamental and deep-going upheavals than political revolutions in that they are attempts, above all, to transfer economic assets and power, and social and political status and privileges, from one social group to another. Consequently, social revolutions tend to be much more violent than political revolutions – especially as the dominant economic and social elites have so much more at stake. The Paris Commune of 1871 and the Russian Revolution of 1917 can both be seen as examples of social revolutions.

What begins as a political revolution can develop – sometimes only briefly – into a social revolution. When it does, it nearly always results in violent conflict between different revolutionary groups. This happened in both the French Revolution of 1789 and in the 1848 revolutions.

Social revolutions tend to happen when a particular economic and social system is seen as having stagnated, or as being incapable of any further progressive development. In such situations, revolutionaries argue that only a fundamentally new type of social system will enable humanity to progress. In fact, they often argue that failure to effect such a revolution runs the risk of a regression to barbarism.

Revolutionary stages

Many revolutions, if they last long enough, seem to pass through at least three distinct phases.

First stage

In the early stages, revolutions usually go in the directions desired by those revolutionaries who have been most active in pressing for changes in the preceding years. In the main, crowds tend to take action in support of the demands of such revolutionaries.

Second stage

If unrest continues despite early revolutionary gains, a second – more radical – stage begins to unfold. Crowds tend to press for changes more specifically in their own interests, and they become increasingly independent in their demands. At the same time, new revolutionary leaders and groups begin to emerge, who demand that the revolutionary process be widened and deepened. Very often, the early leaders of the revolution now come to be seen as too conservative, and are replaced by more radical ones. Sometimes, these changes of leadership are effected by revolutionary purges and terror – especially if a violent counter-revolution is threatened or is already in progress.

At times, the original direction of the revolution can be deflected into areas never desired by the revolutionaries who helped spark off the original revolution. Such aspects can be seen in the French Revolution between 1792 and 1794, the later stages of the 1848 revolutions, and the Russian Revolution from March 1917 to July 1918.

Third stage

A third stage frequently develops after the more radical second stage: here, the fact that revolutionaries remain in power means they have to deal with the practicalities of government. At the same time, the revolutionary energy and idealism which helped fuel both the early and the more radical phases begin to dissipate – as it is not possible to maintain such heightened levels of enthusiasm and activity indefinitely.

In such circumstances, more administratively-minded leaders come to the fore to consolidate the revolution. In this phase, the more radical aspects are sometimes rolled back, and the revolution reverts to its original aims. (It is possible to see the post-Thermidorian developments in France after 1794 as just such a third stage; see pp. 102–3.) Sometimes, leaders in this more conservative phase can begin unwittingly to undermine even the more moderate gains of the revolution, in part by stifling mass involvement and initiative, and so engendering apathy and alienation. Trotsky and his supporters, for instance, began to argue as early as 1933 that a new political revolution against the Stalinist bureaucracy was needed in the Soviet Union, in order to safeguard against the possibility of the restoration of capitalism.

Overview

In the course of this book, all the main ingredients and features of revolution will be examined. To begin with, the important long-term preparatory work of economic, social, political and ideological developments prior to revolution will be explored. Though these are essential if a revolution is to break out, it will be shown that such objective preconditions, factors and triggers are, separately or even in combination, insufficient.

Consequently, equally important subjective factors will also be dealt with, especially the relative roles and actions of crowds, parties and leaders, and the responses – or lack of responses – by existing authorities and counter-revolutionaries.

Finally, the radicalising impact of revolution will be treated, both *within* borders, with a separate chapter on women and revolution, and *across* borders, with a look at the international and global inspiration frequently provided by revolution.

2

The old order undermined:
social and economic developments

Introduction

Most societies change gradually over time – often very considerably. In particular, most *economic* changes usually have considerable *social* consequences. Examples of such changes and developments include:

- rapid changes in population totals;
- significant internal migration (e.g. from rural to urban areas);
- important developments in agricultural or industrial technologies;
- fluctuations in the wealth of different social groups or classes;
- wider access to education;
- improvements in communications.

If these changes and developments are sufficiently severe, extensive or prolonged, a society will periodically experience some sort of crisis. The more rapidly a society changes (whether such changes are seen as positive or negative), the less stable it is likely to be, and the more serious the crisis will be. However, this certainly does not automatically lead to a revolution, with its resulting change in the holders of political, economic and social power.

More specifically, economic crises often result from attempts at rapid internal reform and government incompetence, as well as from any changes in the world or regional economy which might have a negative effect on a domestic economy. However, it is important to remember that a society usually falls into revolution, not when the economic and social situation continually deteriorates, but when a bad situation begins to improve, as people begin to feel more confident about the prospects of changing the status quo.

Though economic crises and rapid changes in the social structure can cause widespread unrest, the situation only becomes revolutionary when these changes combine with political and legitimacy crises – these will be examined in Chapter 3 (see pp. 20–21). However, on their own, social and economic crises do not result in revolutions.

The French Revolution, 1789

Though several historians, such as Robert R. Palmer, have argued that the French Revolution should be seen as part of a broader 'Atlantic' or 'Democratic' revolution which affected several European countries before and after 1789, it is clear that the general crisis of the *ancien régime* in western Europe was most acute in eighteenth-century France.

Society

On the surface, French society seemed a stable social pyramid, with the king at the apex, and beneath him the three feudal orders or estates*:

- First Estate (clergy);
- Second Estate (nobility);
- Third Estate (the rest of society, including merchants, financiers and professionals, as well as peasants and urban workers).

However, the situation was far from static, and some social developments undoubtedly contributed to eroding some of the system's foundations. The orthodox (and often the Marxist) view of the French Revolution tends to stress the importance of social and economic factors as causes of the Revolution. From the 1960s though, alternative or 'revisionist' interpretations have in large part rejected the traditional idea of conflict between a declining nobility and a rising bourgeois or middle class.** Concentrating on local rather than national studies, they have focused on those nobles who became successfully involved in industry and finance; and have stressed that many of the bourgeoisie accepted the values of the nobility, desired the same privileges, and were thus not opposed to the nobility.

While wealthier members of the bourgeoisie continued to be able to purchase titles of nobility in order to obtain high positions in the state, it is nonetheless still possible to see the beginnings of an 'aristocratic reaction' in which the nobility attempted to preserve their feudal privileges and to resist all government attempts to reform the taxation and administrative systems. An example of this, which undoubtedly angered the wealthy sections of the bourgeoisie, was the 1781 Ségur ordinance relating to the army, which restricted commissions to those who could prove four generations of nobility. This was particularly true of members of the liberal professions, who came increasingly to resent their exclusion from a political and social status which they believed was merited by their growing prosperity and improved education.

In addition to tensions between and within the Second and Third Estates, there were also divisions between the higher and lower clergy in the First Estate. A particular tension existed over the bigger proportion of the tithe which was taken by the higher clergy, who were often the younger sons of the most important noble families. These frustrations of the lower clergy can be seen in their *cahiers de doléances* of 1789.

---

* Estates were different social groups of the feudal stratification system. Originally, social movement between such groups was rigidly forbidden, but over the centuries some mobility took place.

** Although many historians begin to talk about classes from the late eighteenth century onwards, a modern class system did not really develop in Europe until the mid nineteenth century, or even later.

REVEIL DU TIERS ETAT.

Ma foute, il étoit tems que je me réveillasse, car l'oppression de mes fers me donnoit le cochemar un peu trop fort.

In this cartoon, a man representing the Third Estate is shown breaking free from his chains. Comment in detail on the message the cartoonist is trying to convey.

Population

During the eighteenth century – especially the second half – France experienced a dramatic increase in population. It rose from 22 million in 1705, to 26 million in 1780, and to 28 million in 1789. This caused particular problems for the peasants, who were by far the most numerous section of the Third Estate. Although most peasants in France had some land, it was frequently insufficient to live on, and the population increase from 1700 made this much worse because of the tradition of splitting holdings between sons.

   The intense land-hunger amongst peasants came at a time when many of them were becoming increasingly angered by their tax burdens, and by the revival of ancient feudal rights by many noble landowners. Furthermore, many landlords were adopting more modern techniques, such as enclosures, which encroached on the peasants' traditional rights of gleaning and pasture. Thus, in general, most peasants experienced a worsening of their conditions from 1765. Increasingly, especially during times of economic crisis, many of the poorer peasants and agricultural labourers drifted to the larger towns, including Paris.

Economic developments

Though France experienced significant growth in overseas trade and colonial expansion in the eighteenth century, the domestic economy experienced considerable problems. Many of these can be linked to the four wars fought between 1733 and 1783, which not only ruined the Crown's finances, but also created inflationary pressures that affected all social groups.

In addition, French agriculture became relatively less productive in this period, leading to frequent food shortages and high prices. However, though the worst large-scale famine was in 1709, and the worst decade was the 1740s (with the years 1741–42 being particularly severe), there were many crises before 1787, often resulting in riots and uprisings, such as the 'Flour War' of 1775.

At the same time, the living and working conditions of urban workers also tended to stagnate or even deteriorate (often made worse by the arrival of large numbers of rural poor); and prices for food and fuel tended to rise much more quickly than wages: between 1726 and 1786, prices rose by between 35% and 65%, while wages rose by only 22%. Furthermore, French industry began to fall behind that of Britain, with recurrent recessions in the textile trade, for instance, in the 1770s. Industry, in general, was particularly hit by the effects of competition after the Anglo-French Free Trade Treaty of 1786. This resulted in even more unemployment, and a consequent increase in disturbances in 1786 in textile centres such as Lyons, Amiens and Rouen, and especially in Paris.

Crisis years, 1787–89

Despite the frequency of these uprisings, none of them was revolutionary. For instance, the sans-culottes of Paris usually responded to times of shortage and hardship by demanding reductions in the price of bread, rather than increases in wages. However, they do indicate a high level of economic dissatisfaction. On top of this simmering unrest, there then followed two years of poor harvests and consequent food shortages, with the price of wheat doubling in two years and reaching record levels in 27 out of the 32 generalities. In towns and villages, wage earners and peasants were forced to increase their daily expenditure on bread to impossible levels, thus further fuelling a widespread but sporadic popular revolt in many regions of France that had been building up in the years before 1787.

The harvest of 1788 was particularly bad, and an unusually severe winter saw thousands thrown out of work in the towns, as increased expenditure on food led to a drop in the sale of manufactured goods. Added to these problems were those created by the thousands of rural poor who flocked to Paris.

The result, by December 1788, was a nationwide revolt against food shortages and rising prices, which continued to spread till the summer of 1789, when there was another bad harvest. By August 1789, the 'Great Fear' of the peasantry was in full swing in the countryside of several regions, where rumours of an aristocratic counter-revolution, with émigrés leading bands of brigands, led to peasant attacks on châteaux and the burning of manorial and feudal charters. At the same time, in Paris, there were the Réveillon Riots. In all of these, food prices continued to play an important role even though, relative to the shortages of the 1740s, the problems of 1787–89 were less intense. Nonetheless, by August 1789, workers were having to spend some 90 per cent of their wages on bread.

On their own, these outbreaks of popular unrest, like those of the 1770s, would not have led to revolution, as they were limited to essentially economic questions. What turned them into revolution was the fact that they coincided with the severe financial problems of the Crown, and the beginnings of a political revolt by, first, the nobility and, later, the members of the Third Estate. These political crises will be examined in Chapter 3.

The 1848 revolutions

The states affected by the 1848 revolutions – France, the Habsburg Empire, and the German and Italian states, for example – had significant differences in their social and economic structures. On a broad scale, western Europe had few large landed estates, peasants were legally free, and there existed a large and increasingly confident middle class. While in central and eastern Europe, land ownership remained concentrated in the hands of the nobility, serfs were still common, and the middle class was relatively much smaller and weaker.

However, over and above each state's specific circumstances, there were some common features – not least of which was the fact that, by 1848, Europe was still mainly rural, with relatively few people living in large cities.

Society

One significant development in nineteenth-century Europe was the clear emergence and rise of an increasingly dynamic middle class, based on industry, commerce and the professions. This trend was discernible before the French Revolution of 1789 but was accelerated by increasing industrialisation, and it continued after the revolutions of 1848. Though it is necessary to bear in mind that the landed classes continued to exercise considerable power in central and eastern Europe, the experiences and growth of the middle classes led them, in most parts of Europe, to demand reforms.

It is also important to realise that the middle classes ranged from an upper middle class of wealthy bankers, industrialists and senior civil servants, to the professional middle class, made up of lawyers, doctors, journalists and university teachers, down to a lower middle class, consisting of shopkeepers, school teachers and clerical workers. Varying in size from state to state, the upper middle class often criticised the weaknesses of existing banking and credit systems, while the professional and lower middle classes (the vast majority) increasingly resented the fact that their educational qualifications failed to bring them the social status and employment they desired, and that their heavy burden of taxation often brought no right to vote. These frustrations about employment and political participation were often most keenly felt by the growing population of students and newly qualified professionals who frequently played an important role in the revolutions of 1848.

Population

As well as the growth and development of certain social classes, another strain on the societies of post-1815 Europe was the rapid expansion of population. This pressure had been emerging since the mid eighteenth century: in 1750, the population of Europe was approximately 130 million; by 1840, this had more than doubled to about 266 million. Most of this was rural rather than urban growth, and it put great pressure on food supplies. By the 1840s, many parts of Europe were clearly overpopulated. Not only was the food supply often inadequate, there was also an increasing problem of underemployment amongst the poorer sections of the rural population. During the nineteenth century, many were forced by economic pressures, such as food shortages and high food prices, to migrate to urban centres, either seasonally or permanently. As a result, many of the rural poor came into contact for the first time with political ideas such as liberalism and even socialism.

Economic developments

Clearly, the most significant economic phenomenon to affect Europe before 1848 was the early stages of industrialisation. It did affect the middle classes, but the impact of this economic transformation was most keenly felt by urban workers. However, industrialisation only became really significant in the latter half of the nineteenth century, and it is important to note that, even by 1848, Europe was still overwhelmingly rural, and there was no automatic link between developing industrialisation and revolution. For instance, the two most industrialised countries in Europe were Britain and Belgium, yet neither of these had a revolution in 1848.

Nonetheless, in the years before 1848, the slow process of industrialisation in countries such as France or in the German states led to a rise in the number of factory workers, who frequently experienced similar living and working conditions. In France, real wages for industrial workers declined overall in the years between 1817 and 1848; while in the German states, the average decline was as high as 25 per cent. Their poor, and often declining, living conditions made them prone to disease, and frequently resulted in social problems such as drunkenness and crime. Particularly worrying for the middle classes was the fact that many states witnessed a growing number of strikes and other forms of urban unrest in the 1830s and 1840s.

However, the factory workers were considerably outnumbered by the artisans, who, though better off than most factory workers, were often hit hard by industrialisation and laissez-faire capitalism. This resulted in the weakening or outright destruction of their guilds, while competition from factory products led to a fall in income and frequent unemployment. In addition, worse problems were created by overpopulation and the frequent fluctuations in food supplies. Better educated than most factory workers, these artisans were often more militant and radical, and played a big part in the revolutions of 1848, in cities ranging from Paris to Vienna.

Also affected by the spread of capitalist methods was the rural population. In particular, small independent peasants in western Europe were often squeezed down into the ranks of rural labourers or the unemployed by laws which, for instance, eroded traditional communal grazing rights. This led to considerable rural hardship and discontent, especially in France, and often radicalised a normally conservative section of society.

Crisis years, 1845–48

As we have seen, by the mid-1840s many parts of Europe had witnessed years of hardship and conflict in both rural and urban areas, as a result of population growth, industrialisation and urbanisation. However, the economic crises reached new heights in the years after 1845: in particular, most parts of Europe experienced a series of poor and often disastrous harvests in 1845 (the potato crop) and 1846 (cereals). This led to high food prices, which badly affected most peasants and artisans, as well as the urban and rural poor. As food prices took a greater share of an already inadequate income, the demand for manufactured goods fell, leading to serious levels of urban unemployment.

The result in many parts of Europe was an increase in the number of food riots, unrest in the larger towns, and frequent attacks on new machinery, which was held responsible for increased unemployment. In most European states, the crisis point was reached in 1847 and, by the spring of 1848, after a relatively better harvest, the worst of the crisis was over. In many areas, food prices began to fall. In the German states, for instance, price levels almost returned to pre-1845 levels, and industrial production and employment began to pick up. The revolutions of 1848 thus took place at a time when economic conditions were generally improving. This underlines the fact that, on their own, economic factors do not lead to revolution. Significantly, the worst hit areas during 1845–47 (such as the Dutch provinces and Belgium) were not the most revolutionary in 1848. On economic factors alone, 1847 should have been the year of revolution, not 1848. What turned these economic factors into revolution was a combination of other factors, which included financial crises and consequent bankruptcies; ineffective relief measures by most governments, which led to them losing legitimacy in the eyes of many social groups; the growth of radical demands for political reform; and, lastly, a loss of dynamism and political nerve by many regimes in the face of these problems and demands.

The Paris Commune, 1871

Unlike the two revolutionary upheavals already examined, the Paris Commune of 1871 was much more clearly the result of a particular crisis in one year, linked to the specific problems of war and defeat. However, there were nonetheless some long-term social and economic factors which contributed to the Commune's specific features.

Society

The hopes of urban workers in France, following the revolution of 1848, had been largely disappointed. A second workers' insurrection in Paris in June 1848 had been easily suppressed, and conservatives had dominated French politics till 1851. To some extent, Louis Napoleon had attempted to introduce policies to benefit all social groups, including some to improve the living and working conditions of urban workers. However, several of his attempted reforms had been blocked by the Council of State and local administrators. Nonetheless, from 1852 to the mid-1860s, some wage earners experienced a rise in their standard of living, with wage increases mainly keeping pace with prices. This, however, related more to the skilled minority of workers than to the unskilled majority who, for most of the second half of the nineteenth century, saw few significant improvements. From the mid-1860s, a check in living standards eventually led to a series of strikes in 1869–70.

Population

While, overall, France's population growth in the nineteenth century was lower than that of countries such as Britain and Russia, or the states of Germany and Italy, significant developments were taking place in Paris itself. There, by 1871, much of Paris's population (which rose by over half a million in the years 1850–71) consisted of rural immigrants who often found it hard to adjust to life and work in a large city. Many of them, in fact, merely exchanged unemployment in the countryside for unemployment in a city. This increase in the city's population caused real problems for living conditions. Though the social reforms of Louis Napoleon alleviated some of the worst problems, the gap between rich and poor in Paris tended to increase in the years before 1871. This was, at least in part, due to strong reluctance on the part of conservative politicians to increase taxes in order to pay for improvements in the living conditions of the masses.

Economic developments

During the period 1852–70, there was a steady increase in industrialisation in France, and considerable economic growth. However, the benefits of this prosperity were unequally divided, with the commercial classes obtaining the lion's share. Once the living standards of urban workers began to stagnate in the 1860s, a feeling of bitterness began to grow.

Crisis year, 1871

Despite certain problems which had begun to build up by 1870, France was by no means in a revolutionary situation. The Commune of 1871 was clearly linked to exceptional circumstances in Paris itself – hence the failure of attempts to spread the *commune* movement to Lyons and Marseilles. It was France's sudden defeat in the Franco-Prussian War, 1870–71, the harsh peace terms of the Treaty of Frankfurt following that defeat, the political divisions in France, and the economic hardship during and after the siege of Paris (see pp. 63–64), that led to this attempted revolution. The war itself had caused great economic dislocation, which was only increased by the terms of the Treaty.

During the war and the siege, many businesses had closed as a result of lost access to raw materials and customers. Unable to find work, many Parisians had responded by not paying their rent, by pawning the tools of their trade, and by joining the Parisian National Guard, which paid a small daily wage. At the same time, shopkeepers resorted to a system of credits.

However, a new National Assembly, elected in February 1871 and headed by Adolphe Thiers, decided that there should be a rapid return to economic normality and, in the following month, voted to stop these practical emergency methods used by the citizens of Paris to cope with the hardship of the siege of Paris, which had begun in September 1870. This led within days to thousands of bankruptcies and therefore to large-scale unemployment.

This came on top of the National Assembly's decision to move to Versailles, rather than to return to Paris from Bordeaux, where it had been meeting since its election in February 1871. This was due partly to the conservative Assembly's distrust of the more radical and republican capital, and partly to Thiers' fear of 'the vile multitude', which he clearly linked with social and political unrest. Although Thiers vastly overrated the amount of revolutionary unrest in Paris, it was clear he was determined to force a showdown.

This came on Saturday 18 March 1871, with a provocative attempt to remove over 400 cannons still under the command of the National Guard of Paris. The reaction of the angry crowds gave Thiers the excuse he was looking for, and his decision to recall all political officials and civil servants from Paris made possible the creation of the Commune.

The Russian Revolution, 1917

The Russian Revolution of 1917, like all revolutions, was a complex upheaval involving social and economic, as well as political, factors. This revolution is a particularly graphic illustration of how even progressive changes can so seriously undermine the foundations of a society that, when a deep crisis (often external) appears, the entire structure is prone to collapse.

Society

In the half-century before 1917, Russia was still in many respects semi-feudal when compared with countries such as Britain, France and Germany. According to the census of 1897, over 85 per cent of the population were still peasants; serfdom, in fact, had only been abolished in 1861. Even at the turn of the century, in law Russia's people still belonged to one of four 'estates' (nobility, gentry, townsmen or peasants). This made no provision for new social groups such as the professional middle class or industrial workers. Officially, membership of one of these estates was fixed at birth but, from the late nineteenth century onwards, mobility between the estates was possible. One significant factor was the expansion of education, which resulted in a large number of educated Russians, including a growing subgroup of students, who saw themselves as part of a classless intelligentsia with a duty to bring about an improved society. Together, they came increasingly to resent their lack of political rights under the semi-feudal Tsarist system.

Population

The break-up of this old social structure was in part due to an explosive population growth, which began in the eighteenth century but accelerated in the nineteenth, increasing by 300 per cent between 1815 and 1900. This was due to an increased birth rate, as the death rate in Russia actually rose between 1891 and 1900 – an indication of the poor living conditions experienced by the vast majority of the population. One result, despite the emancipation of the serfs in 1861 and the agricultural reforms of Peter Stolypin from 1906 to 1911, was a severe land-hunger amongst the peasants. Though they experienced no marked improvement in their economic position from 1875 to 1914, they did not suffer any significant deterioration either. However, many continued to suffer from heavy burdens of debt, and their tradition of subdividing their holdings did nothing to reduce the pressure of land-shortages, which continued right up to the revolution of 1917. In addition, there was also a steady increase in the number of poor peasants and landless agricultural labourers.

Economic developments

Though relatively backward in many ways, the Russian economy in the late nineteenth century was far from static. Following Russia's defeat in the Crimean War, 1853–56, Tsar Alexander II had encouraged industrial expansion and, in the latter half of the century, Sergei Witte (minster of finance 1893–1903) had carried out further industrialisation with the aid of capital and technical assistance from western European countries such as Britain, France, Belgium and Germany. This economic growth, known as the 'Great Spurt', led to a significant increase in Russia's national wealth, and to improvements in its banking and credit systems. The years 1890–99 and 1907–13, in particular, saw rapid growth rates in industrial production; and between 1861 and 1913, the average annual growth rate was almost 6 per cent.

This industrial expansion had been assisted by a world-wide boom in the 1890s. However, the boom came to an end by 1900 and was replaced by a recession in international trade which, in turn, led to high unemployment and increased social unrest in Russia. Though the situation began to improve after 1908, high inflation and lagging wages in Russia meant unrest continued to simmer.

Russia's industrial expansion in this period before 1914 also contributed to instability by creating a social group which was to be central in the overthrow of Tsardom: the industrial working class. From only a few hundred thousand in the 1890s, the number of permanent industrial workers increased rapidly to almost 3.5 million by 1914. More significantly, the introduction of relatively modern technology in late-nineteenth-century Russia led to a high concentration of workers in large factories. By 1910, the proportion of workers in factories employing more than 500 was nearly 54 per cent – the corresponding figure for the USA was 33 per cent. These workers were also concentrated in a few major centres such as Kiev, Odessa, Moscow and St Petersburg. Their working and living conditions were terrible – often similar to the most appalling conditions found in the early industrial revolution in western Europe. Forced together, in large numbers, their bitter resentment boiled over into large-scale strikes, and made them particularly receptive to revolutionary ideas in the years 1890–1917.

Crisis years, 1914–17

While there were thus many sections of Russian society who had serious social and economic grievances, Russia did not seem (even to Lenin) to be on the verge of revolution in 1914. It was the economic impact of Russia's participation in the First World War which helped push Tsarist Russia from a crisis into a revolution.

In particular, the economy (already relatively backward compared with those of its western Europe neighbours) was devastated by the strains of three years of total war. This had disastrous repercussions on all sections of society, but especially on the peasants and the industrial workers.

In the countryside, the backward agricultural system, deeply dependent on manpower and horses, was deprived of both, as these were increasingly drafted to the front lines. After just two years of war, with over 15 million men and over 60 per cent of horses removed from farming, the system began to crumble. In addition, the war destroyed the financial stability which had existed before 1914, and resulted in high inflation rates far outstripping peasant incomes and making trading unprofitable. Consequently, peasants began to reduce their sales of grain and, instead, began to hoard it or to use it for vodka.

In the towns, the peasants' reluctance to sell added to the pressure on food supplies created by the size of the army, which, by 1917, was over 36 million strong. Daily bread rations dropped from 2.7 pounds in January 1916 to 1.8 pounds in March 1917. Furthermore, the strains of war disrupted the transport system to such an extent that, by 1916, the railway network was on the point of collapse. This meant that it was increasingly difficult to send what limited food there was even to major urban centres such as Moscow and Petrograd. On top of this, growing inflation led to many firms going bankrupt, with a resulting increase in unemployment, while those still in work saw their real wages drop by as much as 30 per cent in 1917 alone. As social unrest increased, in the form of strikes and food riots, fearful factory owners shut down their factories and fled, thus adding to the problems of unemployment and hunger in most major cities.

It is thus not surprising that these long-term and short-term social and economic developments before 1917 gave Russian revolutionaries a far bigger audience than they had ever had before.

Pre-revolutionary France, 1776–89

2.1 The purchase of nobility and its privileges

A. R. J. Turgot, controller-general of finances 1774–76, writing in 1776

There is no rich man who does not become noble and as a result the body of noblemen includes all the rich men and the controversy over privileges is no longer a matter of distinguished families against commoners but a matter of rich against poor.

Source: D. Townson, *France in revolution*, London, 1990, p.15

2.2 An Enlightenment view of the *corvée*

A. R. J. Turgot, from the preamble to his Edict on the corvée *(1776)*

To take the time of the labourer, even for pay, is the equivalent of a tax. To take this time without paying for it is a double tax, and one out of all proportion when it falls on the simple day-labourer who has nothing for his livelihood but the work of his hands.

The man who works under compulsion and without payments works idly and without interest; he does less work, and this work is badly done. Those who perform the *corvée* are forced to travel often ten miles or more to report to the foreman, and as much again to return to their homes, and so waste a good part of the time demanded from them without any return for it.

Source: E. G. Rayner and R. F. Stapley, *The French Revolution, 1789–99*, London, 1995, p. 13

2.3 The feudal obligations of the peasantry

A. Besnard, writing about the village of Les Alleuds in Souvenirs d'un nonagenaire, *in 1880*

As to *lods et ventes*, the acquirer of a property not only had to hand over to him an authentic copy of the deed of acquisition which the feudal lord was entitled to keep for a year and a day, during which time he could decide either to receive these dues or to exercise a withdrawal, that is, to keep the property for himself, at a cost of reimbursing the acquirer for genuinely incurred expenses. He also had the privilege of handing his right of withdrawal to anyone he pleased.

Source: J. Lough, *An introduction to eighteenth century France*, London, 1980, p. 100

2.4 A contemporary view of the causes of agricultural prosperity . . .

Arthur Young, a famous English writer on agriculture, who visited France just before the 1789 Revolution

'July 30 1787
Going out of Ganges, I was surprised to find by far the greatest exertion in irrigation which I have yet seen in France; and then pass by some steep mountains highly cultivated in terraces. Much watering at St Laurence. The scenery very interesting to a farmer. From Ganges to the mountain of rough ground which I crossed, the ride has

been the most interesting which I have taken in France; the effect of industry vigorous; the animation the most lively. An activity has been here that has swept away all difficulties before it and has clothed the very rocks with verdure. It would be a disgrace to common sense to ask the cause; the enjoyment of property must have done it. Give a man the secure possession of a bleak rock, and he will turn it into a garden; give him a nine year lease of a garden and he will convert it into a desert!'

Source: C. Maxwell (ed.), *Young, travels in France during the years 1787, 1788, 1789*, Cambridge, 1929, p. 47

2.5 ... and agricultural poverty

Arthur Young, a famous English writer on agriculture, who visited France just before the 1789 Revolution

'Sept. 5 1788

To Montauban. The poor people seem poor indeed; the children terribly ragged, if possible worse clad than if with no clothes at all; as to shoes and stockings they are luxuries. A beautiful girl of six or seven years playing with a stick and sinking under such a bundle of rags as made my heart ache to see her. They did not beg, and when I gave them something seemed more surprised than obliged. One-third of what I have seen of this province seems uncultivated, and nearly all of it in misery. What have kings and ministers and parliaments and States to answer for their prejudices, seeing millions of hands that would be industrious, idle and starving, through the execrable maxims of despotism, or the equally detestable prejudices of a feudal nobility.'

Source: C. Maxwell (ed.), *Young, travels in France during the years 1787, 1788, 1789*, Cambridge, 1929, p. 109

Document case-study questions

1 Describe *briefly* the privileges which noblemen in France had before 1789, as referred to by Turgot in Document 2.1.
2 From what you have read in this book and elsewhere, explain the following references: (a) *corvée* (Document 2.2), (b) *lods et ventes* (Document 2.3).
3 How useful are Documents 2.1, 2.2 and 2.3 as historical evidence for explaining peasant grievances in pre-revolutionary France?
4 Assess the reliability of Documents 2.4 and 2.5 as evidence of the problems of French agriculture before 1789.
5 How far do these *five* documents explain the social and economic discontents in France in the period 1786–89?

Political crises and revolution

Introduction

As previously noted, from time to time all societies experience economic and related social crises of varying degrees of seriousness. However, though such crises can result in prolonged and sometimes violent unrest, they are unlikely, in themselves, to lead to revolution. For this to happen, other elements are needed: one of these is the political dimension. Several common features of political disagreement and conflict are present in most revolutions.

Important factors contributing to the creation of political crises include:

- Unpopularity of particular rulers and politicians, often accompanied by popular anger at specific policies – foreign policy and especially war (which always tests the structures of a society in a particularly intense way) can be of crucial importance.
- Suspicion or exposure of scandals and corruption, or growing dissatisfaction with administrative inefficiency.
- Divisions within the ruling political elites, either among members of the government, or among those dominant groups normally supporting the regime.
- Inconsistent or hesitant policies, especially belated attempts at reform. These often, ironically, lead to *greater* opposition, and create a political vacuum, giving opportunities for wider public debate and broad alliances involving groups other than the political elites.

Such political crises, as with economic and social crises, can come and go without ever resulting in a revolution – even if they occur in combination. However, if they are prolonged and are not resolved to the satisfaction of a significant proportion of the population, political conflict is more likely to turn into revolution. In such circumstances there may be a general collapse of social and political consensus, and a consequent loss of faith in a society's total political system – what some historians (and other social scientists) refer to as a 'crisis of legitimacy'.

In such a crisis, as large sections of the population increasingly lose respect for political leaders and institutions, thereby calling into question the established order or status quo, panic (as well as divisions) can develop within the ruling elites. As a result, the machinery of the state becomes paralysed and thus unable to take effective action against opposition and unrest. If the crisis of legitimacy is deep enough, the forces of law and order (police, army) will become more and more unreliable, creating the potential to transform a pre-revolutionary situation into a revolutionary one. These features will be seen frequently as this chapter examines each revolution in turn.

The French Revolution, 1789

Of the many factors which contributed to the outbreak of revolution in France in 1789, the impact of war, and unpopular foreign policy, played a major role.

The economic problems, rising social tensions and growing administrative problems of the *ancien régime* were undoubtedly made worse, in political as well as economic terms, by French involvement in the Seven Years' War, 1756–63, and in the American Revolutionary Wars, 1778–83. As a consequence, France was on the verge of financial collapse. As early as 1781, after being dismissed as controller-general of finances, Jacques Necker had published his *Compte rendu*, exposing the size of the royal deficit. This led to widespread public discussion and outrage, with strong political criticisms of royal ministers and of the personal extravagance of Marie-Antoinette. By 1786, the debt stood at 110 million livres – an increase of 300 per cent over that of 1776. Thus the debt and bankruptcy resulting from these wars significantly weakened the French monarchy. Later on, the threat of invasion and war pushed the French Revolution in ever more radical directions and into new political crises, including the end of the monarchy as an institution; the execution of Louis XVI; and the political struggles between Girondins and Jacobins in 1792–93.

In addition, there was also growing dissatisfaction with Louis XVI's foreign policy, especially the failure and humiliation of his Dutch policy in 1787, and France's apparent diplomatic slide into the position of a second-rate power. Significantly, the Dutch fiasco seriously weakened army morale less than two years before the outbreak of revolution. It was against such a background that Louis decided, in February 1787, to convene an Assembly of Notables to approve a radical programme of financial reforms, including a reduction in the taxation privileges of the social elite who made up the Assembly. However, this initiative for financial reform, begun by the Crown in 1787, and necessitated by the costly wars, resulted in a series of political crises during the next two years, which finally began the French Revolution in 1789. It was Louis' ministers, such as Charles-Alexandre de Calonne and Loménie de Brienne, who made the various proposals for a reorganisation of the tax system, including a universal land tax, which provoked so much opposition from the nobles. The first crisis developed in February 1787, when the Assembly of Notables refused to accept the suggested reforms, and Calonne made an open appeal for public support. The political conflict between nobles and the Crown moved from the Assembly to the *parlement* of Paris, and other *parlements*, with a prolonged period of political turmoil lasting from May to August 1788, known as the Revolt of the Aristocracy, during which Brienne's reforms were also rejected.

The nobles, determined to maintain their privileges and distinctions and unable to come up with any compromise, would only advise the government to make economies. The Crown began to lose the political initiative. Finally, in desperation, in August 1788, Louis made the fateful decision to call a meeting of the Estates-General (a national political institution which represented the three Estates), which had not met since 1614. This can be seen as having far more political significance for the development of the French Revolution than the storming of the Bastille.

This refusal by the aristocracy to co-operate with royal suggestions for reform is evidence of growing political divisions amongst sections of the social and political elites of France. Continuing beyond the Assembly of Notables and the *parlements*, such divisions were even more pronounced in the Estates-General, which met for the first time on 5 May 1789. As the conservative reaction continued, preventing the emergence of any political compromise, several members of the First and Second Estates began to break ranks: Honoré Gabriel Riqueti, Comte de Mirabeau, and Emmanuel Joseph Sieyès (known as Abbé Sieyès) had already stood for election to the Third Estate, while others, such as Marie Joseph Paul Motier, Marquis de Lafayette (commander of the French army, 1778–83, during the American War of Independence) clearly favoured some reforms. By 27 June, about 50 nobles and a clear majority of the clergy were sitting with the Third Estate, which had declared itself to be a National Assembly and, on 20 June, had taken the Tennis Court Oath not to disperse until a new constitution had been granted.

These political divisions were present even within the royal family itself: on the one hand, Louis' cousin, the Duc d'Orléans (later known as Philippe-Egalité), was a radical who helped undermine Louis' position, and even voted for his execution in 1792; while on the other, Louis' brother, the Comte d'Artois, opposed any reduction in royal power. Such divisions made trust and compromise with the opposition much more problematic, weakened the Crown, contributed to contradictions and paralysis, and so gave revolution more of a chance.

However, the aristocratic resistance and political divisions also contributed to the spread of political discontent and agitation beyond the traditional elites who, as in other eighteenth-century European nations, were normally united in supporting royal authority. The effect of their divisions was to undermine the mechanisms of political control in France during 1789. Though the aristocracy saw the calling of the Estates-General as their victory, there were widespread discussions surrounding the elections and the drawing-up of the *cahiers de doléance*. Though the *cahiers* themselves were not particularly radical, the public political space grew to involve members of the lower orders – not just in Paris, but also in the provinces. Since 1749, there had been a growing loss of royal control over local administration, with local *parlements*, from the 1750s, increasingly taking their political lead from the *parlement* of Paris. As public discussion of national political problems widened after 1787, royal administration collapsed even more. This, in turn, encouraged the participation of many social groups previously excluded from political activity. More significantly, the political expectations of such groups were dramatically increased.

When he became king in 1774, Louis XVI was already aware of mounting political tensions, and had displayed hesitation and contradiction from the beginning. In 1774, he sacked Louis XV's unpopular minister, René Nicolas Maupeou; recalled the *parlement* of Paris; and appointed the first of a series of reforming ministers. Yet he then refused to support the reforms of Anne-Robert-Jacques Turgot, controller-general of finances, dismissing him in 1776. As the political crisis deepened from 1787, his hesitation and indecision increased. In the critical year of 1789, as political control mechanisms continued to collapse, and sections of the population became increasingly radicalised, the reactions of Louis and his ministers became more and more confused and contradictory. In particular, after the events of June 1789, he seemed to waver between acceptance of a new constitution, and attempts at a royal counter-revolution – a clear example of panic and lack of resolution in a revolutionary situation.

The 1848 revolutions

The French Revolution of 1789, with its ideals of liberalism and republicanism, and its stimulation of nationalism, had unleashed political turmoil in Europe. For example, the reactionary Vienna Settlement of 1815 was a clear attempt to reassert the authority of the *ancien régime* in the face of what was to be the ever-present spectre of revolution. This conservatism, particularly associated with Austria's chief minister, Clemens von Metternich, was triumphant during the wave of revolutions between 1820 and 1824 but, from 1829 onwards, began to lose control during a second wave which ended in 1834. Fourteen years later, within weeks of the publication of Karl Marx and Friedrich Engels' Communist Manifesto, on 24 February 1848, what has been called the 'Springtime of Peoples' had begun: a wave of revolutions rolling on from France, through Austria, Bavaria and Prussia, and on to Italy.

Nineteenth-century liberalism was based on the belief that government should be conducted with the consent of all the propertied and wealthy sections of society. Hence liberals favoured reducing the property qualification for the franchise to include the lower middle classes. They also wanted economic reforms such as free trade and the ending of feudal restrictions, as well as making political demands for free speech and freedom of the press. Radicalism, on the other hand, went beyond liberalism in being more democratic – in particular radicals argued for universal manhood suffrage, believing that rich and poor alike should have the right to vote. Unlike liberals, who favoured constitutional monarchy, radicals usually supported the creation of a republic.

Nationalism also grew in importance in the nineteenth century, based as it was on the belief that people sharing a common language, history or culture should be able to rule themselves in their own nation states. Nationalism came to be an increasingly potent force in the Habsburg Empire and in the German and Italian states. In many cases, it was closely associated with liberalism.

By 1848, political power throughout Europe was still in the hands of conservative or reactionary regimes, mainly devoted to the interests of small, privileged and disproportionately wealthy elites. Yet, in many states in 1848, there developed in capital cities massive anti-regime demonstrations (with varying political demands), followed by rapid capitulation on the part of the rulers because of their initial panic and the unreliability of troops. Initially these uprisings came about when liberal nobles, bourgeois professionals, students and even urban workers and peasant farmers united in demanding liberal and constitutional reform. Increasingly dissatisfied with government economic policies, they joined together to form broad opposition fronts. We will look at the specific aspects of political crises in three areas: France, the Habsburg Empire, and the German states.

France

Though not quite the first revolution of 1848 (there was a revolt in Sicily in January 1848), the overthrow of Louis Philippe on 24 February became an example for reformers and revolutionaries across Europe, and helped set off a rapid revolutionary chain-reaction across most of Europe. By 1848, the regime of Louis Philippe, which had come to power in 1830, was losing political credibility. Between 1831 and 1839 there had already been several uprisings against the July Monarchy. In the 1840s, political opposition turned to the parliamentary arena, where there was particular hostility to the chief minister, François Guizot, an arch-conservative who was closely tied to policies favoured by the king and who dominated French politics from 1840, becoming prime minister in 1847.

Guizot's election victory in 1846 caused him to become complacent about growing political opposition, and he further undermined the position of the regime by his corrupt attempts to maintain his majority. The middle classes were also alienated by the discovery of various financial scandals (such as the *affaire Petit*), which were widely reported. Political confidence in the regime was further weakened by unpopular foreign policies, such as the decision to become involved in the Spanish Marriages Question, and what was seen as an unpatriotic reluctance to follow a policy of colonial expansion.

From March 1847, attempts to extend the very limited franchise to wider sections of the middle class were defeated by Guizot, and led to the Banquet Campaign to extend the right to vote, which began in July 1847. This took the political debate about reform into a wider public arena, with particular effect on the increasingly discontented lower middle classes: from November 1847, following the Lille Banquet, the campaign included calls for social reform and even a republic. A third attempt to extend the franchise on 12 February 1848 also failed, saw moderate leaders such as Thiers lose control to radicals, and brought together a broad alliance of those who desired to overthrow the regime.

The banning of a protest banquet on 22 February led to large demonstrations, and these events persuaded Louis Philippe, at last, to dismiss Guizot. However, this concession came too late. When some nervous troops fired into the crowd, the protests turned into a riot, with over 1,500 barricades quickly erected in Paris.

What turned this into a revolution was the action of the National Guard: essentially middle class and alienated, they either joined the demonstrators, or just refused to disperse the crowds. This weakened ability of the regime to repress the people and to reimpose order, and the large demonstrations, caused the upper-middle-class supporters of the regime to lose political courage. As in 1789, a breakdown of elite support led to political retreat and a power vacuum, thus giving an opening for more radical opponents. Louis Philippe abdicated, and the Second Republic was established.

Habsburg Empire

From 1815 to 1848 there had been almost total political stagnation, with chief minister Metternich operating tight political control and ignoring the need for reform. As was the case in France, however, political movements emerged, demanding liberal constitutional reform. Yet, from 1830, weaknesses and divisions within the political elite became apparent: these were present even within the imperial court itself, after the ambitious Count Francis Kolowratz was put in charge of imperial finances. A bitter rival of Metternich's, he, like many, thought Metternich had been in power too long, and had prevented his own political rise. Certainly, Metternich became increasingly unpopular, and less dynamic and successful. Furthermore, when Francis I died in 1835, to be replaced by the mentally impaired Ferdinand, the rivalry between Metternich and Kolowratz in the new *Staatskonferenz* reduced the effectiveness of the government and resulted in mounting political inertia. In particular, civil service plans for reform were ignored, at a time of growing social and economic changes.

In Vienna, middle-class liberal opposition found allies amongst more liberal sections of the lower nobility, and when news of the February Revolution in France reached Vienna in March, this broad alliance was encouraged. Led by intellectuals such as Alexander Bach and Alfred Lohner, who remained loyal to the Habsburg dynasty, their demands included extension of the franchise, constitutional reform, and the dismissal of Metternich. The divided and paralysed court quickly assented – on 13 March, Metternich was forced to resign and, on 14 March, censorship was lifted and a manifesto promised a new constitution. Events were even more dramatic in Hungary, where large demonstrations in Budapest, and the political unreliability of the garrison's Italian conscripts, resulted in a new liberal government.

German states

As in France, the rise of liberalism in the German states reflected the growing political dissatisfaction amongst the middle classes. There had been various demonstrations and riots in 1830, following the July revolution in Paris; but, from then until 1848, Metternich had successfully persuaded the German states to stand firm against liberal and nationalist demands. In the south German state of Bavaria, the 1848 revolution was sparked off by a political scandal relating to King Ludwig I's mistress, Lola Montez. She was an Irish dancer, and was consulted by Ludwig on political matters. His decision to make her a countess, and to request she be given Bavarian nationality, led to a political crisis and divisions amongst the governing elite. His ministers resigned en bloc, but a new cabinet gave in to his demands. Outraged students from the university of Munich organised massive demonstrations in protest, and in February 1848, attacked Lola Montez's house. Ludwig responded by closing the university, but when news of the revolution in Paris reached Munich, the demonstrations grew larger, with many demanding a republic. The business and professional classes, desiring political participation and a more liberal state, were also alienated from the regime. Having already fatally weakened the position of the monarchy, Ludwig belatedly banished Lola, and then abdicated in favour of his son, Maximilian.

In the more reactionary north German state of Prussia, where the Junkers (landed aristocracy) were the ruling class, Frederick William IV headed a powerful absolute government. However, Frederick William had a contradictory attitude to liberalism and, in February 1847 – against the express advice of Metternich – had called a United Diet (a limited parliament), with the power to approve taxes in order to pay for the construction of a railway from Berlin to the economically important areas of east Prussia. When this Diet opposed his plans for increased taxation, and instead raised strong liberal demands for a constitution, Frederick William refused to make concessions. Though he dissolved the Diet in June 1847, discontent had been stirred, and the political confidence of the regime had been shaken. Liberal hopes were rekindled by news of the February Revolution in France and, on 18 March 1848, news of Metternich's forced resignation reached Berlin. Clashes between protesters and troops, coming on top of the earlier political pressures, were enough to lead Frederick William to promise some reforms. However, crowds celebrating in the streets of Berlin were fired on by panic-stricken royal troops. In the so-called March Days which followed, widespread demonstrations and the erection of barricades forced the king to withdraw his troops and to allow the crowds to arm themselves. Frederick William was (if only temporarily) frightened into granting reforms, and appointed a liberal ministry on 29 March. As in the other states, weakness and confusion amongst the elites at crucial political moments, coming on top of various social and economic crises, resulted in rapid capitulations.

The Paris Commune, 1871

Though war was to prove crucial in turning political crisis into incipient revolution in 1871, political divisions had already been undermining Napoleon III's Second Empire regime. Rising to power on the back of liberal and conservative fears following the revolution of 1848, Napoleon III's middle-class supporters had soon turned critical. From 1859 to 1861, he had declared a political amnesty and had relaxed press censorship, but this attempt to defuse opposition had the opposite effect. From 1863, when 35 opposition deputies were elected, the critics were strengthened and political conflict deepened. The elections of 1869 resulted in an even stronger opposition and, by the spring of 1870, Napoleon III (already seriously ill) was convinced that only significant liberal concessions would avert 'the peril of revolution'. Despite winning the plebiscite on his proposed 'Liberal Empire', the unity of the political elites continued to crack, as the middle classes experienced economic difficulties.

There was also growing opposition to the regime's foreign policy interventions. There had been the tragic Mexican expedition, 1861–67; the failure to benefit from the Austro-Prussian War, 1866–67; and the inconsistent interventions in Italy, which angered the Catholic church and prevented the creation of an alliance with Italy and Austria. By 1870, not only had Napoleon III left France dangerously isolated, but these foreign policy failures had resulted in growing internal disillusionment, and declining political support for his regime.

The actual decision to become involved in a war with Prussia in 1870, which increased the political pressures and widened the cracks in political unity to breaking point, was taken more by his ministers – especially the incompetent foreign minister, the Duc de Gramont, and the prime minister, Emile Ollivier – than by Napoleon III himself, who, by then, was fatally ill. Essentially, this government was too weak in the Assembly to risk any diplomatic humiliation at the hands of Otto von Bismarck.

The war itself was a disaster: within a month, the French had been forced to surrender at Sedan, and Napoleon III was captured. When news reached Paris, the intervention of the Paris crowd allowed moderate republicans in the Assembly to set up a Government of National Defence, thus sweeping aside the newly appointed Regency Council. Unfortunately, it had little support, even amongst the political elite. More seriously, the Prussian victories continued, as this new government's prosecution of the war was timid and half-hearted, fearing as it did the likely political implications of a revolutionary mobilisation of the masses. Meanwhile, in Paris – which had suffered months of hardship because of the Prussian army's siege – the political situation became more tense, with sections of the National Guard, and other groups, demanding the election of a Commune by universal suffrage. Alarmed, the new government responded by closing down the political clubs and, finally, formally surrendering to the Prussians on 28 January 1871.

Serious political divisions now opened up in France over peace or war, a republic or a return to monarchy: the new Assembly, elected on 8 February, was mainly composed of conservatives, royalists and moderate republicans. This new Assembly refused to proclaim a republic and instead instructed Adolphe Thiers to make peace: the harsh peace terms made the political situation even more revolutionary in Paris which had returned many socialists in the recent elections. On 15 March, the National Guard created a Republican Federation, controlled by a central committee of 60. On the same day, a new Commune was elected, with some 60 per cent either members of Marx's First International or supporters of the anarchist Auguste Blanqui. Three days later, on 18 March, the insurrection of the *communards* began, following the government's decision (under Prussian pressure) to disarm the National Guard and remove cannons from Paris. The resulting armed clashes turned a revolt into a revolution. By 28 March, Commune control of the city had been established.

The Russian Revolution, 1917

As with the Paris Commune, the March and November[*] 1917 revolutions in Russia were the result, ultimately, of war – in this case, the First World War. Furthermore, as in France in 1789, the first steps in this deepening political crisis were taken by those amongst the political elite who had rallied to support the Tsar on the outbreak of war in 1914. There had been no political reform in Russia to match economic changes, or the demands of the professional middle classes and the students who desired participation in the political process. As a result, the political and administrative machinery of Tsarist Russia was fragile, making the regime shaky and vulnerable to any crisis. The defeats suffered by the Russian troops, and the war itself, put massive and ultimately fatal strains on the undemocratic Tsarist regime. With Nicholas II away at the front after 1915, confusion and scandal arose around Gregori Rasputin, who had a close friendship with the Tsarina, and who used his influence to promote or demote members of the government. Though he was murdered in December 1916, his behaviour had greatly damaged the regime. In particular, the political elite (including the propertied classes and officer corps) began to withdraw their support, in the face of Nicholas II's refusal to dismiss incompetent ministers or create a cabinet with wider national support. By 1917, most of them were too weary or too angry to attempt to save him.

Equally significant was the growing unreliability of the troops. As the demonstrations and strikes – begun by women workers on 8 March to mark International Women's Day – spread and developed into a general strike, the police and Cossacks began to disintegrate. Ominously, the Petrograd garrison became unreliable, with many units fraternising with the demonstrators. Unable to disperse the crowds, the authorities became paralysed and many of the Tsar's ministers fled from the capital. This political vacuum increased after the highest-ranking generals persuaded Nicholas II to abdicate, with the attempt to establish a constitutional monarchy failing when Grand Duke Michael refused to accept the crown. Thus, Tsardom collapsed from within, and Russia became a de facto republic.

However, the indecision and hesitation at the top remained in face of the continuing militancy of the masses. A self-appointed provisional committee of the duma (parliament) – itself elected on a very narrow franchise before the war – set up a provisional government. Yet the crisis of legitimacy continued as this provisional government had no electoral mandate and, more importantly,

---

[*] Before the Bolsheviks took power, Russia used a calendar which was 13 days behind the one used in the rest of Europe. Hence, according to the old calendar, the first revolution in Russia took place at the end of February; according to the modern calendar, it was early March. Similarly, the Bolshevik revolution took place on 25 October (old calendar), or 7 November (modern calendar). To avoid confusion, the modern calendar has been used throughout.

decided to continue Russia's involvement in the war. Lacking political legitimacy, with no supporting legislative body, this provisional government rested on the tacit consent of the army high command. Of particular significance was the rebirth of another political institution, on the same day: the Petrograd Soviet. (A soviet was a workers' council or strike committee.) Initially, the idea was that these two bodies would work together – the popular element co-operating with and supporting the elites in the provisional government. Yet, as war minister Alexander Guchkov observed from the beginning, the Soviet's famous Order Number 1 effectively undermined the provisional government's control of the armed forces.

From March to November 1917, there was thus a situation of dual power – an uneasy political truce, in which the authority of the provisional government crumbled day by day. As the pressures of war continued, and the army disintegrated, the political gulf between these two bodies widened. Furthermore, elements of class conflict developed, radicalising the increasingly militant factory workers and rank and file soldiers. One significant political result was that the Mensheviks and Social Revolutionaries – the more moderate socialists who initially dominated the Petrograd Soviet – lost their seats to the Bolsheviks and the even more militant anarcho-syndicalists. These political groups were not prepared to keep in power an unelected government which refused to end Russia's involvement in the hated First World War.

This political vacuum, initially masked, became increasingly exposed, as the rulers moved further to the right in face of the growing radicalisation of the masses. More and more out of step with the public, the provisional government experienced one political crisis after another, with frequent ministerial changes, and hence became increasingly discredited. The failure of the June offensive on the Galician Front further alienated the Petrograd Soviet, created new tensions with the military leaders and resulted in the resignation of Prince Georgi Lvov and the liberal Kadet (Constitutional Democrat) ministers in early July. By then, the March compromise between the elites and the popular movements crumbled as the middle ground in politics all but disappeared. Though the provisional government was able to survive the crisis of the July Days, the new prime minister, Alexander Kerensky, faced an increasingly tense situation, with rumours of either a left-wing rising, or a right-wing coup. The right were the first to move, when General Lavr Kornilov, newly appointed as commander-in-chief by Kerensky, attempted a coup in late August. This proved disastrous for Kerensky who, in a state of panic and paralysis, was forced to rely on the Bolsheviks and their Red Guards. Their resolute and successful actions gave them substantial election victories in September, both in town and city councils and especially in the soviets, where they won a majority in Petrograd (13 September) and in Moscow (19 September).

Encouraged by these victories, Lenin was eventually able to persuade the Bolshevik central committee to begin organising the final overthrow of the provisional government, whose authority was clearly breaking down. Kerensky's growing isolation was shown by the failure of his pre-parliament, and his inability to form a new government. He was further discredited by the continued reluctance to honour promises to call an election for a constituent assembly which would give the Russian people their first democratically elected and accountable government. As the political crisis deepened, the provisional government became more and more nervous of the likely results. Significantly, however, since the March revolution, Russia had become an extraordinary political arena, with wide public debate and participation. In both urban and rural areas, soviets were established: these not only raised political demands, but often became de facto administrative bodies, thus adding to the impotence of the various provisional government bodies. Elections to these soviets were frequent and the All-Russian Congress of Soviets was the only nationally elected body in Russia which could – and increasingly did – claim to speak for the people as a whole. As the provisional government failed to deal with food supplies, transport, law and order and army organisation, the soviets moved to fill this political vacuum.

In rural areas, Kerensky's refusal to deal with the land question until after the war built up pressure for an immediate political solution, resulting in rural soviets and individual peasants beginning their own land expropriations. While in urban areas, lock-outs, closures and flights by employers led to workers seizing the factories and establishing their own factory committees. By the autumn of 1917, Kerensky's government was almost totally isolated, and existed in name only; a directory (i.e. a small, non-elected government) appointed in September was replaced by another short-lived coalition cabinet in October. In the end, Kerensky was left with a nominated cabinet which had little support from left or right, and which ominously had little effective military backing. The Bolsheviks thus did not so much overthrow his regime in November 1917, as merely step into the political vacuum left by the growing process of collapse.

The role of ideology

Introduction

Despite their undoubted importance, pre-revolutionary factors such as social discontent, economic hardship and political crises – even in combination – are not enough to make a revolution. What is further required, in order to give these general dissatisfactions some clear revolutionary direction, is something to give cohesion to the often widely varying frustrations and aspirations of different social groups.

One key additional factor which needs to be present is ideology: a set of related and coherent ideas and principles about what is wrong with the present situation *and* about how the world could and should be in the future. Ideologies are thus normally the product of intellectuals, and perhaps the clearest example of an ideology produced by an intellectual is that of communism, as developed by Karl Marx.

Some Marxist historians tend to stress social and economic developments as being more crucial, as these allow the emergence of corresponding ideas. However, the connection between ideologies and revolutions is not always a clear one. In particular, sets of ideas do not often have their greatest effect at the time of their formulation – they frequently only become widely accepted at a very much later date. Furthermore, ideologies developed in one country often find it easy to cross borders – especially at extraordinary times – and can thus have a wider regional and even global impact.

If social-economic and political crises persist for any length of time, many people begin to re-examine traditional ways of thinking. Increasingly, as a deepening revolutionary situation develops, people begin to discuss new or different sets of ideas as possible solutions. At such times, almost everyone becomes a sort of intellectual – even those who would normally hardly ever think about economics or politics. It is precisely in such situations that an ideology can provide a common language of protest and a unifying body of ideas. Indeed, an ideology can be compared to a piston which gives force and direction to the otherwise ineffective 'steam' of general discontents. The historian George Rudé called this a 'common revolutionary psychology'.

It is this potential power of ideas and ideologies which has led most regimes to resort to censorship in one form or another, especially since the revolutions of the eighteenth and nineteenth centuries. One result has been that would-be revolutionaries have increasingly attempted to spread their ideologies through revolutionary parties; but the importance of these will be examined in Chapter 5.

The French Revolution, 1789

Although there was no clear and unified ideology in France before 1789, by 1794 the French Revolution had brought to the forefront most of the ideologies and concepts which still influence political thought today. The list includes: self-determination, nationalism, democracy, the sovereignty of the people, equality, and even aspects of socialism.

Although it offered no coherent programme of political change, it is generally accepted that the French Revolution was both directly and indirectly influenced by an intellectual ferment which had been affecting almost the whole of Europe since the late seventeenth century. This ideological background to 1789 is known as the Enlightenment.

1740–70

While most of the main texts of the Enlightenment had been published by 1750, it is possible to argue that, at the least, the criticisms and attacks by such Enlightenment writers (or *philosophes* as they were generally known) as Montesquieu and Voltaire on the superstitions and abuses of the *ancien régime* did much to weaken its traditional supports. However, it is important to stress that most of the main figures of the Enlightenment were only concerned to challenge and reform the accepted traditions, values and institutions, not to overthrow them. For instance, Montesquieu's *L'Esprit des lois* (1748), which argued that monarchical despotism was prevented by the privileges of other groups who shared political power, could be used in defence of the nobility, as well as making a case for the Third Estate.

In fact, the Enlightenment in France was more radical and influential than in any other country. From the 1740s, when it began to be more significant, it was an intellectual movement which stressed the need for rational and critical thought to be applied to all aspects of life. Of particular significance were the writings of Jean-Jacques Rousseau, especially his *Contrat social* (1762), with its references to direct democracy and the 'general will' of the people.

However, historians dispute the extent to which these writings were known outside the circle of intellectuals in the salons of Paris. In the 1790s, writers such as Edmund Burke blamed the revolution on the subversive writings and plots of the *philosophes*. Although Alexis de Tocqueville rejected this conspiracy theory, he nonetheless claimed that these writings of the Enlightenment had helped undermine the *ancien régime* by exposing and ridiculing its weaknesses. Yet it is difficult to be clear on the extent of the Enlightenment's spread in France before 1789. For instance, Arthur Young noted the relative absence of newspapers, and the fact that political reading was not as widespread as he had imagined it would be.

Nevertheless, from the 1750s, the *parlements* began to justify their opposition to royal ministers such as Maupeou, and what they called 'ministerial despotism', by reference to the works of Montesquieu, Rousseau and other *philosophes*. This deliberate attempt to mould public opinion in order to gain support for the *parlements'* struggles against the Crown had the effect of spreading key Enlightenment ideas to the ranks of the urban poor, if not to the peasants. These tracts and remonstrances of the *parlements* thus helped prepare the ground for more radical ideas in the 1780s.

Also very important in spreading the ideas of the Enlightenment was the production of the *Encyclopédie* by the philosophers Diderot and d'Alembert, in 1751–72. The intention was to summarise the whole of human knowledge but, at the same time, its 28 volumes helped popularise radical Enlightenment ideas – Diderot, d'Alembert and Helvétius often wrote in glowing terms in their contributions of the virtues of republicanism. Though the *Encyclopédie* was very costly to buy, by 1789, some 25,000 sets had been sold across Europe. In 1779–80, a cheaper edition was so popular that over a hundred printing presses were needed to meet demand. By then, there was beginning to emerge a clear consensus of general principles amongst a reasonably coherent social group, and this later allowed effective revolutionary unity in the 1780s and 1790s. In particular, it made possible a rapid transition from a collapsing *ancien régime* to a new revolutionary one.

1770–95

This slow spread of Enlightenment ideas was accelerated by the political and economic crises of the 1770s and 1780s. One significant influence which gave impetus and currency to such ideas was the American War of Independence and the establishment of the new republic. Soldiers returning to Europe, and especially to France, brought with them the new ideals of republicanism, democracy, and the rights of man. As the crises developed in France before 1789, a host of writers and pamphleteers, such as Jacques Pierre Brissot de Warville (usually referred to as Brissot), produced a flood of tracts and journals critical of the authorities – their slogans were increasingly popularised by street-corner orators who thus introduced them to the urban poor. These appeals to the opinion of a public usually excluded from politics also led to the formation of political clubs.

Louis XVI's decision to call a meeting of the Estates-General, against this background of ideological debate and ferment, finally gave an opportunity for the rights of the Third Estate to be formulated. This was done by people such as Abbé Sieyès and the Comte de Mirabeau: during 1788 and 1789, political terms such as citizen, social contract, the nation, liberty, fraternity, and the rights of man, filtered down, below the 'literacy line', to the lower social groups in Paris, and formed the background to the abolition of feudalism and the Declaration of the Rights of Man and of the Citizen.

However, the influence of the *philosophes* of the Enlightenment did not stop in 1789. After the declaration of the republic in 1792, new ideologies and programmes for action began to emerge, such as Jacobinism and Hébertism. Maximilien Robespierre and Louis Antoine de Saint-Just, in particular, were much influenced by the writings of Rousseau; and though the Jacobins in the period 1793–94 in many ways departed from the idea of a strong legislative, a weak executive, and a separation of powers, this can be explained as distortions resulting from the extreme dangers of war and civil war after 1792. Also, it has been said that Robespierre and the Jacobins merely accentuated some of the more authoritarian aspects in the writings of Rousseau, for example, the idea of the 'virtuous few' legislating in the interests of the 'general will'.

Though only about 50,000 of France's population of 26 million in 1789 could be said to be strongly 'enlightened' – the extent of royalist and counter-revolutionary sentiment after 1789 suggests that the spread of radical Enlightenment ideas was certainly not universal – it would be fair to say that the *philosophes* of the Enlightenment undoubtedly contributed to the spirit of revolt that began to affect all of Europe, and especially France, in the period 1770–90. Moreover, as we shall see, a significant legacy of the French Revolution of 1789 was to be a set of ideas that were to re-appear in all subsequent revolutions up to the Russian Revolution of 1917, and even beyond, to the Chinese students in Tiananmen Square in 1989.

The 1848 revolutions

The French Revolution of 1789 had at least weakened, if not destroyed, the idea of monarchs being demi-gods and political systems being unchangeable. This was true especially but not exclusively in France. After all, the largest army in Europe had been unable, in 1789, to prevent the unfolding revolution in France. It also gave a pattern for future revolutionaries to follow in all subsequent revolutions, including those of 1848, 1871 and 1917. However, despite some attempts after 1815 to move some way towards more representative government, most European regimes were still conservative and relatively absolute in 1848. Yet, during the 1820s and 1830s, some of the ideological seeds of the French Revolution began to germinate and flourish. The two most important for the revolutions of 1848 were liberalism (political and economic) and nationalism. Also developing, but at a slower rate, were democracy and socialism.

As early as 1819, in the Carlsbad Decrees, the Austrian and Prussian monarchies had attempted to control the spread of liberal ideas in the German states. Nonetheless, these ideas continued to simmer and, by 1830, there appeared to be a genuine revival of the revolutionary movement in many parts of Europe. So much so, in fact, that many of the political elites began to feel that the tide of history was against them. By January 1848, de Tocqueville made a speech claiming: 'We are sleeping on a volcano . . . A wind of revolution blows, the storm is on the horizon.' One effect of these developments and reactions was that the ruling elites, who had already begun to fear the return of the revolutionary disorder and violence of 1789, were often initially undecided as to how to act in the face of the early protests of 1848, and this made them impotent.

One important factor in the spread of liberalism and nationalism – both of which were especially associated with the expanding middle classes of the nineteenth century – was the expansion of higher education. In the first few decades of the century, many new universities had been created in the capital cities. There was thus a much larger body of students. These, and also many of their university teachers, were to make many universities into centres of political radicalism, and students were often to play a significant part in the revolutions of 1848 – which had not been the case in the French Revolution of 1789. In large part this was because, as state bureaucracies increased in size after 1815, many young men came to expect state employment, on the basis of the 1789 ideal of a 'career open to talent'. Thus, from 1815 onwards, many intellectuals continued to hope for the eventual triumph of the ideals of 1789.

At the same time and, in part, connected with the earlier expansion of education, the 1830s and 1840s witnessed a tremendous growth – despite censorship problems – in the numbers and circulation of newspapers, periodicals and pamphlets, though this was mainly in western Europe. Aided by new printing technologies, such as the use of steam, the most modern presses could print thousands of relatively cheap copies an hour. Many were devoted to spreading the ideas of liberalism and nationalism, which included demands for a constitution, an extension of the franchise, the ending of press censorship, various civil rights and, where relevant, self-determination or national unity. Liberals also demanded the end of feudal rights and restrictions, and the establishment of a freer economy. The result by 1848 was the creation of a large and informed educated middle-class public opinion on a range of political issues. Although the conservative ruling elites undoubtedly overestimated the spread and strength of these ideologies, they nonetheless were a significant cause of the paralysis of governments which was to be seen in the revolutions of 1848, which will now be examined separately.

France

The ideological currents stemming from 1789 were probably strongest in France. Salon liberals, while rejecting the more revolutionary democratic traditions of 1789, nonetheless were to the fore in demanding constitutional reforms, such as an extension of the franchise to the middle classes. In particular, liberals were the prime movers in the Banquet Campaign, which finally brought about the overthrow of Louis Philippe in February 1848. In Paris, in particular, a radical and often republican liberal tradition developed, demanding manhood suffrage. In 1830, this had led to a revolution which forced Charles IX to abdicate.

While liberalism was clearly the dominant current in France by 1848 – as it was elsewhere in Europe – it is important to note other ideological developments between 1815 and 1848. Especially significant for future European – and world – history was the emergence of revolutionary democratic and socialist currents. Developing from the Hébertists of 1793–94 and François (Gracchus) Babeuf in 1796, French socialism began to construct an ideology based on popular, democratic power and to create economic, as well as political, equality. By the

1830s, a conspiratorial tradition (based on the ideas of Claude Saint-Simon, Proudhon, and Blanqui) was contributing to political turmoil in France: 1831 saw a socialist uprising in Lyons, while 1839 saw the great Parisian revolt which inspired Victor Hugo to write *Les Misérables*. Many of the elites were worried by the number of pamphlets attacking private property – Proudhon's *What is property?* (1840) caused particular concern. Though these ideas spread amongst urban workers throughout the 1830s and 1840s, they were less significant than liberal ones in the 1848 revolution.

German states

Here, since 1815, the liberal and democratic ideas of 1789 had been kept alive by the universities. More than the 1848 revolution in France, those of 1848 in the German states can thus be seen as revolutions by the intellectuals and the educated middle classes. In 1830, following news of the revolution in France, there had been demonstrations and riots in several of the larger states, some of which resulted in the granting of constitutions in Saxony, Brunswick and Hanover, during the years 1831–33. These, however, were limited and still essentially conservative, and thus failed to satisfy liberal demands. From 1839, liberal leaders from several German states met at annual joint conventions to discuss future plans and, until 1848, liberal demands for constitutional reforms continued to grow.

This was especially true of Prussia, where the towns were often very liberal. Liberals there wanted constitutional reforms and a liberal–national merger of German states. When Frederick William IV disappointed liberal hopes in 1840 by his half-hearted reforms, opposition strengthened, helped by the new and cheaper printing technologies, and by the railways and the telegraph, which aided the spread of their ideas. Further setbacks over the Estates-General in 1847, followed by news of the February 1848 revolution in France, led to the demonstrations which prompted Frederick William to grant a constitution and civil liberties. In this March revolution, the students and teachers of the University of Berlin played an important role, even forming their own armed corps. While, in Hesse, students of the university of Giessen acted as the main leaders of the insurgents.

However, these liberal movements were ultimately weakened by the fact that many liberals were also nationalists: many of them placed more importance on national unity than on political reforms. Also, most liberal movements had little or nothing to offer the emerging movement of artisans (or *Handwerker*) and factory workers. These divisions made it easier for the various rulers to eventually reassert their authority.

Habsburg Empire

The ideological contributions to revolution were more confused here. While in Austria, there were middle-class liberal demands for reforms such as manhood suffrage (votes for all men) and a constitution, elsewhere, especially in Hungary and Czechoslovakia, there were also demands for national freedom and the

Ana Ipatescu, a young Romanian radical, leads a demonstration in 1848 to demand independence from Hungarian and Russian rule. How might these demonstrators have drawn inspiration from the French Revolution?

abolition of feudal remnants. For liberals, as well as for nationalists, the struggle for self-determination against the old autocracies could be seen as part of the same struggle, as these regimes were also the enemies of liberalism. All these liberal and nationalist demands increased from 1835 to 1848 during the Vormärz period (i.e. before the March revolution of 1848). Such sentiments were especially strong in the towns. In the March 1848 demonstrations in Vienna that led to the resignation of Metternich, the lifting of press censorship, and the granting of constitutional reforms, students played an important part. Their Academic Legion, about 5,000 strong, later sparked off the radical upheaval on 26 May, after the government attempted to disband it.

Italian states

There was widespread liberal agitation throughout the area for constitutional reform, but, as in the German states and the Habsburg Empire, there was also the current of nationalism which opposed the rule of the Austrian Empire. In 1831, there had been various risings, led by secret societies such as the Carbonari, mostly for internal constitutional reforms. Their failure led Giuseppe Mazzini to reconcile the ideals of liberalism and nationalism, and to form a new secret society: *Giovine Italia* (Young Italy). This organisation grew in membership throughout the 1830s and 1840s, and its ideas were widely read. Mazzini's *Duties of man* gave Italian nationalists a simple but coherent philosophy with which to challenge the authorities.

The election of a new pope, Pius IX, in 1846 also contributed to the revolutions here in 1848. A known liberal, he almost immediately, in 1847, granted some

37

liberal reforms, including introducing the limited Consulta (a council of state, with some secular representatives, to share decision-making) and ending press censorship. By January 1848, there were almost a hundred newspapers in Rome. With some liberal reforms also granted in Piedmont and, after a rising in February 1848, in Naples, by March 1848 only the Austrian parts of Italy were without some form of representative government. Hence a strong combination of liberal and nationalist feelings was directed against Austrian rule after Metternich's fall.

The Paris Commune, 1871

As we have seen, the revolutions of 1848 were, in the main, a reflection of the ideologies of liberalism and nationalism. However, another ideological strand, which was largely disappointed in 1848, was that of socialism, with its call for social and economic, as well as political, reforms. In France, this had led to the rising known as the June Days. Though brutally crushed, this emerging socialist movement continued to grow, especially under the more liberal phase of Napoleon III's rule after 1859.

However, despite the fears of the political elites and the subsequent writings of Karl Marx, it would be wrong to see the Paris Commune of 1871 as essentially inspired by the ideology of late-nineteenth-century socialism – despite the strong egalitarian and co-operative elements in many of the Commune's acts. In fact, several different ideological currents contributed to the establishment of the Commune in March 1871. The strongest – and the majority one, as far as the March elections were concerned – was liberal republicanism, though this was mainly its more radical and populist variety, many of whose adherents tried to reproduce some of the Jacobin aspects of 1792–94 in the months March–May 1871 (see p. 49). In large part, this was because the Commune should be seen more as a response to war, invasion and perceived treachery than as a revolution inspired, like those of 1789, 1848 and 1917, by specific ideologies with clear and coherent political ideas.

Nonetheless, there were other, more revolutionary, political ideologies which also influenced the direction of the Commune, although their adherents never had overall control. Of these minority currents, the most important was socialism, though not really of the utopian variety, which had suffered a sharp decline after the 1848 revolutions. There were two main, and more revolutionary, varieties in the Commune of 1871. Firstly there was Blanquism, a revolutionary form of socialism based on the ideas of Blanqui which played a significant part in the Commune. Like the members of the First International, however, they too, were a minority: winning almost one third of the seats in the March elections. Much influenced by the Hébertist and Jacobin traditions of 1793–94, Blanqui's followers believed a small conspiratorial group of revolutionaries could bring about the desired future by organising an armed *coup d'état*. Consequently, the Blanquists often acted in alliance with the radical Jacobin republicans, and between them, they won 57 seats. Though there were, by 1871, thousands of revolutionaries in Paris who were opposed to the current system, many of whom were members of the various political clubs, they remained a minority in 1871.

The other major socialist strand was that of the adherents of the International Working Men's Association (generally known as the First International), which had been founded in 1864, largely under the guidance of Karl Marx. Marx had deliberately used the term 'communism' to mark the clear difference between this strand of socialism and utopian socialism. In the March elections, almost one-third of the delegates elected were members (17) or supporters (5) of this First International, though they only held 4 out of the 90 seats on the central committee. Yet only one member of the Commune, Leo Frankel, was truly a Marxist. The socialism of these French followers of the First International, developed mainly by Marx and Engels after 1848 (but also influenced by left-wing Proudhonists led by Eugène Varlin), was an ideology which they believed explained the historical process, and which aimed at a decentralised federal system of *communes*, with a variety of socialist and egalitarian reforms. Convinced by Marx's theories, many of them no doubt believed they were involved in the beginnings of a socialist revolution, but their views remained those of a minority. However, these followers of Marx and Blanqui did get the Commune to adopt the red flag as the symbol for the *communards*.

Another, minority, ideological influence during the Commune was anarchism, based mainly on the ideas of Pierre Joseph Proudhon and, especially, Mikhail Bakunin. These ideas, too, developed after 1848, especially during the 1860s, and involved a hatred of any system of government and a belief that destruction of the old was essential before the new could be constructed. Though this political current was strong enough to help cause the split and eventual collapse of the First International in 1872, and was to spread to many countries – especially Spain – in the nineteenth and twentieth centuries, it was very much a minority influence in the Commune of 1871. However, the commander of the *communard* forces, Gustave Cluseret, was an officer much influenced by Bakunin, and had been involved with him in an earlier and abortive rising in Lyons.

The Russian Revolution, 1917

Though it is clear that ideology – or, to be more precise, Marxist ideology – was crucial for the November Revolution, there were, in fact, many different ideological strands behind the revolutionary year of 1917. These other currents were, indeed, much more significant than Marxism for the March Revolution.

Liberalism

Of these other ideological components, liberalism was very much the weakest one. Drawing inspiration from the ideals of the French Revolution of 1789, the numerically small and politically weak middle class desperately hoped for a reform of the semi-feudal Tsarist system. In particular, they wanted to see a stronger form of representative government, with full constitutional and civil rights, including the ending of censorship. Initially encouraged by the October

Manifesto and the calling of a duma during the 1905 revolution, they had been increasingly dismayed and frustrated as the Tsar undermined and then ended the duma experiment. By 1917, the main liberal party, the Kadets (Constitutional Democrats), was largely ineffective, and committed to peaceful reform.

Populism

However, there were several other, more revolutionary, ideologies at work in Tsarist Russia in the decades before 1917. From the 1860s to the 1880s, many radical intellectuals, convinced of the futility of requesting liberal reforms from autocratic Tsars, developed the revolutionary populist movement in order to create a liberal political system, with elements of socialism based on the peasants' traditional communal life. They looked to the peasants – whom they tended to idealise – as the revolutionary force in Russia and, in order to become closer to the people, they began the Narodnik experiment in the early 1870s. This involved students moving into the countryside to spread socialism amongst the peasants. Particularly influential in this were the ideas of Alexander Herzen, which gained a significant circulation in intellectual circles as a result of *Kolokol* (*The Bell*), a newspaper which he had begun publishing in 1857. The failure of the Narodnik scheme led his more extreme followers to advocate the use of terrorism as a way of hastening the revolution, in the belief that the assassination of ministers would provoke a severe repression which would, in turn, finally make the peasants rise in revolution. The terrorist group People's Will was thus formed in 1879 but, despite its assassination of several ministers – and, in 1881, even the Tsar, Alexander II – the revolution failed to materialise.

Socialism

Out of these failed populist ideologies there came, in 1901, another political movement which was to play a crucial role in the period before and after the March revolution: the Social Revolutionaries (SRs). Though they tried to widen their appeal by turning to industrial workers, they remained true to their populist roots by being essentially a peasant-based party – despite their commitment, from 1906, to what they called 'revolutionary socialism'. Their main call was for the land to be redistributed or returned to those who worked it, combined with liberal demands for political freedoms and the calling of a constituent assembly. In addition, their populist philosophy was shown by their continued adherence to terror and assassination, which they saw as legitimate political methods.

Marxism

It was the revolutionary socialism of Marxism, however, that was to prove especially important in events after March 1917. Initially, Russian Marxism, like the SRs, had its roots in the populist tradition, in that its earliest proponents – Georgi Plekhanov and Paul Axelrod – had both been associated with the Narodniks. After its failure, these two became attracted by Marx's theories, which identified the industrial working class, not the peasants, as the revolutionary class capable of transforming society. Though the industrial workers were, at the end of the 1870s, only a small minority in Russia, Plekhanov and Axelrod were encouraged by the rapid industrialisation which began under the direction of minister of finance Witte.

They, and many other Russian intellectuals, accepted Marx's idea that socialism could only come about after the development of capitalism had created a modern and prosperous society and economy, with a large (if not majority) industrial working class. Thus the early Russian Marxists did not believe in the possibility of an immediate revolution in Russia. Instead, they saw themselves as having two simultaneous tasks: to assist middle-class liberals in their struggles against feudalism and Tsardom, and to educate the industrial workers for their revolutionary task to come. In 1898, they set up the Russian Social-Democratic Labour Party on clear Marxist principles.

An important reason for the wide appeal of Marxism amongst Russian intellectuals was the absence of any strong liberal tradition in Russia. Consequently, many middle-class Russians saw Marxism as an ideological weapon in their struggle for liberal reforms against Tsarist autocracy. They did not think very much about socialism, which most thought would not be possible for many decades.

This 'legal Marxist' approach (so called because it did not attempt to organise a revolution), however, was based on an oversimplification of Marx's ideas of capitalism as a progressive force in comparison with feudalism and, especially, of his concept of the different stages a society *might* pass through. This over-simplified view became the 'traditional' or 'orthodox' version of Marxism in Russia for many years. Such Marxists believed there would have to be a long, and separate, bourgeois or capitalist stage in Russia's historical development, before there could be any moves to socialism.

It was arguments over this more 'traditional' interpretation of Marx which, ultimately, lay behind the 1903 split in Russia's Marxist party, the RSDLP. One faction, the Mensheviks, stuck to this evolutionary scheme of waiting until all the objective conditions were sufficiently developed to enable a transition to socialism. The other, minority, faction – the Bolsheviks – eventually came to adopt a more revolutionary interpretation: firstly, that (as Marx had said in 1850) it would be difficult in practice to separate the two stages; and, secondly, that as the Russian middle class was too weak and/or reactionary to make a bourgeois revolution, then the workers would have to take power. Thus, by 1917, Lenin had developed a Marxist position very similar to Trotsky's 1905–06 theory of permanent revolution, in which he had argued that, once in power, it would be unrealistic to think that, while carrying out liberal democratic reforms, the workers would not also *begin* to move towards socialism.

Though Bolshevik ideology was to play virtually no part in the March revolution, from April 1917 onwards, it increasingly challenged the Menshevik and Social Revolutionary theories, and, in November 1917, this version of Marxism appeared victorious. Though later events suggested to many that perhaps the Menshevik version was more correct, it is important to realise that, until Lenin's death, no Bolsheviks believed Russia could become socialist on its own.

The role of ideology

Document case study

Revolutionary politics and *communards*, 1871

4.1 The *communards'* determination to resist

Proclamation by the Commune, 22 May 1871

Enough of militarism! No more staff officers bespangled and gilded along every seam! Make way for the people, for fighters, for bare arms! The hour for revolutionary warfare has struck. The people know nothing of intricate manoeuvres; but when they have a gun in their hand, paving stones underfoot, they have no fear of all the strategists of the monarchical school. To arms! Citizens, to arms! It is now a matter, as you know, of either winning or falling into the hands of the reactionaries and clericals of Versailles, of those wretches who have deliberately handed France over to the Prussians, and who are making us pay the ransom for their treachery.

Source: R. L. Williams, *The French Revolution of 1870–1871*, London, 1969, p. 149

4.2 The significance of political clubs and activists in the Paris Commune of 1871

The Government's perception of Paris was not totally incorrect; it was merely exaggerated. There were in the city thousands of political activists who did not accept the prevailing social order and the political system which ensured that the rights of property and the desire to keep taxes low were always given precedence over the needs of the people, especially the need for healthy living and working conditions. These activists had organised themselves into political clubs, at which discussions about the changes that were needed and the way in which they could be best brought about took place. The clubs had even organised themselves into a city-wide federation which held meetings in an attempt – generally fruitless because of passionate disagreements – to co-ordinate their activities. But only a tiny minority of Parisians were members of political clubs. The Government over-rated their importance.

During the Siege almost every able-bodied man had joined the National Guard and a Central Committee of the National Guard had emerged as a vehicle for publicizing the views of the fighting men of Paris. The Government was correct in thinking that this organization had pretensions that outstripped its legal standing, for the Central Committee was dominated by men who hoped to capitalize on the dislocation of war in order to bring about social and political changes. Yet even here it was only a very small minority who were in any sense revolutionaries.

Source: K. Randell, *France: the Third Republic, 1870–1914*, London, 1986, pp. 15–16

4.3 The opposition of Paris to Thiers' peace with Prussia

Socialists in the National Guard and a growing party organized by Blanqui were demanding the election of a commune by universal suffrage. The government closed the political clubs. They had already sent Thiers to the German headquarters to negotiate an armistice.

Paris surrendered on 28 January 1871, and a new assembly was elected on 8 February. In Paris many socialists were returned. The departments under German occupation and the south-east chose republicans, but the rest of France preferred opponents of Gambetta, either Orleanist or Bourbonist. The assembly met at Bordeaux, refused to proclaim the Republic, but elected Thiers, now, at seventy-three, at the peak of his popularity, 'head of the executive power'. His first function was to make peace with Bismarck – a peace which lost France Alsace-Lorraine and its one-and-a-half million people. But in Paris the National Guard had not disarmed, the eastern suburbs were strongly socialist, and the assembly's peace was bitterly resented. A 'Republican Federation of the National Guard' with a central committee of sixty was established on 15 March, and three days later the socialist insurrection began. The mayors of Paris, among them the young Georges Clemenceau, tried to secure a compromise agreement from the assembly, but without success. Alongside the central committee of the National Guard a commune was elected, nearly a third of its delegates being members of the First International, and another third followers of Blanqui. The republican calendar and red flag were adopted.

Source: H. Hearder, *Europe in the nineteenth century, 1830–1880*, London, 1988, p. 204

4.4 Political revolutionaries in the Commune

The only organized body left in the city was the moderate Central Committee of the National Guard, which found itself obliged to take over the essential services, abandoned by Thiers' orders. Naturally those who came to the front in this emergency were the stronger and extremer leaders, bred in the red clubs which had flourished during the siege of Paris. The eternal conspirator, Blanqui, temporarily not the eternal prisoner, had been the inspiring genius of the most famous of the clubs, meeting in the Halles. His *club rouge* has been described as 'a chapel consecrated to an orthodox classical cult of conspiracy, in which the doors were wide open to everyone, but to which one only returned if one was a convert'. Blanqui himself presided over the cult, with 'his delicate, superior, calm countenance, his narrow, piercing eyes shot across now and again with a dangerous, sinister light' – an unusually favourable picture of the conspirator described by Victor Hugo as 'a sort of baleful apparition in whom seemed to be incarnated all the hatred born of every misery'.

The Blanquists were only a tiny fraction, the rest of the Parisian rebels felt the need to legitimise their position by holding elections. A municipal government, to be known by the historic but alarming name of Commune, was elected on 26 March. The name of the Commune was a memory of the year II, of the Jacobins of Robespierre and the sans-culottes of Hébert. It was a symbol beneath which the most opposed schools of revolutionary thought could rally. Four separate groups can be distinguished among its members – the pure revolutionaries, divided between Blanquists and Jacobins, the federalists following Proudhon, and the adherents of the First International. The conservatives or moderates returned in the first election of the Commune resigned, and after complementary elections there was a revolutionary majority of some 57 Blanquists and Jacobins, and a socialist and Proudhonist minority of about 22.

Source: A. Cobban, *A history of modern France, vol. 2, 1799–1871*, Harmondsworth, 1965, p. 212

4.5 A view on how the Commune operated

From Karl Marx, The civil war in France, *read to the general council of the First International on 30 May 1871, two days after the final defeat of the Commune*

The Commune was formed of the municipal councillors, chosen by universal suffrage in the various wards of the town, responsible and revocable at short terms. The majority of its members were naturally working men, or acknowledged representatives of the working class. The Commune was to be a working, not a parliamentary body, executive and legislative at the same time. Instead of continuing to be the agent of the central government, the police was at once stripped of its political attributes, and turned into the responsible and at all times revocable agent of the Commune. So were the officials of all other branches of the administration. From the members of the Commune downwards, the public service had to be done at *workmen's wages*. The vested interests and the representation allowances of the high dignitaries of state disappeared along with the high dignitaries themselves. Public functions ceased to be the private property of the tools of the central government. Not only municipal administration, but the whole initiative hitherto exercised by the state was laid into the hands of the Commune . . .

The multiplicity of interpretations to which the Commune has been subjected, and the multiplicity of interests which construed it in their favour, show that it was a thoroughly expansive political form, while all previous forms of government had been emphatically repressive. Its true secret was this. It was essentially a working-class government, the produce of the struggle of the producing against the appropriating class, the political form at last discovered under which to work out the economical emancipation of labour.

Source: D. Fernbach (ed.), *The First International and after*, Harmondsworth, 1974, pp. 209–12

Document case-study questions

1 What reason can be found in Document 4.1 for the formation of the Paris Commune?

2 From what you have read in this book and elsewhere, explain *briefly* the following references in Document 4.4: (a) Blanqui, (b) Proudhon, (c) the First International.

3 How far do Documents 4.2 and 4.3 agree about the influence and role of political activists and clubs during the Paris Commune of 1871?

4 Assess the usefulness of Document 4.5 as historical evidence of the role played by working-class individuals and organisations in the administration of the Commune.

5 To what extent do these *five* documents support the argument that political ideology was the main inspiration of the *communards*?

5 Crowds, parties and leaders

Introduction

For many, the traditional relationship in the unfolding of revolutions is an essentially top-down model: leaders form and control parties which, in turn, activate and direct the masses. Consequently most histories of revolutions have tended to concentrate on the role of individual leaders and their parties – ranging from Robespierre and the Montagnards to Lenin and the Bolsheviks.

Without minimising the influence and importance of individuals and parties, this chapter will in large part seek to explore the relationship in reverse, by examining the impact of the anonymous individuals who made up the revolutionary crowds. Another aspect to be explored is the degree of opposition that leaders have faced from within their own parties – especially at times of political crisis. However, it is important in general to realise that, until the end of the nineteenth century, 'parties' were much looser ideologically, and less disciplined, than modern political parties.

As we have already seen, great historical processes such as revolutions require favourable objective circumstances, such as economic or political crises. Without these, the subjective actions of individuals and parties are rarely able to have any significant effect. In addition, all major revolutionary upheavals have experienced phases in which revolutionary leaders and parties have been sidelined by the masses moving at greater speed and in more radical directions than the leaders and parties wanted or judged wise.

Nonetheless, leaders and parties are important: there are plenty of examples of when objective circumstances were apparently ripe for revolution, yet no revolution occurred. Often, this was because of the refusal or inability of leaders and parties to take appropriate action or, at times, because of the virtual absence of revolutionary leaders and parties. More interestingly, such inaction sometimes results from a lack of unity between leaders and parties, with one element of the partnership being unwilling to push for revolution by taking advantage of the opportunities briefly thrown up by the haphazard course of events.

While revolutions, especially in their early stages, frequently happen suddenly, they are rarely totally spontaneous. It takes decades of revolutionary ferment, and the slow growth of ideas, to produce the moral and political climate in which a revolutionary overthrow of the old order can be contemplated. Thus, behind any revolution, lie many years of revolutionary endeavour and activities.

It is precisely here that leaders and parties can play crucial roles, by developing critical philosophical, political and economic theories, exploring effective methods of political action, and building close connections with the discontented sections of society. Such revolutionary leaders and parties act like moles during politically quiet periods, burrowing away under the foundations of traditional society, while remaining ready to take immediate action as soon as circumstances change. Leaders and parties thus both help generate, and attempt to direct, revolutionary steam amongst the people, in order to fundamentally transform society.

Sometimes, however, sections of the people, once mobilised into political activity, seek to push the revolution on beyond the aims of the original leaders. This results in conflict and division within the revolutionary ranks, with some either refusing to support further charges, attempting to maintain the new status quo by force, or even moving over to the side of conservatism and counter-revolution. It is this process of revolutions at times devouring their own supporters which has caused real tragedies for many revolutionaries and their parties.

The French Revolution, 1789

Parties and leaders

The political groups which arose during the French Revolution were not really parties in twentieth-century terms. In general, they tended to lack a recognised and coherent political programme, rarely had an organised and consistent membership, and often had few readily identifiable national leaders. Their names, for instance, were often based on their meeting places rather than being indications of their political beliefs – the Jacobins taking their name from the fact that they rented premises from the Dominican friars (nicknamed 'Jacobins'), while the Cordeliers were named after the Parisian electoral district in which they met.

Nonetheless, several reasonably distinct political groups can be identified during the period 1789–95. One thing virtually all these parties and leaders had in common was that they were almost exclusively middle class.

Most famous of all was the Jacobin Club, set up in October 1789, after the Assembly had been forced to move from Versailles to Paris. By July 1790, it had about 1,200 members, most of whom were quite wealthy. By early 1791, they had over 900 affiliated clubs in the provinces. The Jacobins, via their Correspondence Committee, even had an international dimension, as well as a national one. Up to the summer of 1791, they remained reasonably united around demands for a liberal constitutional monarchy. However, the flight to Varennes and the Champ de Mars massacre, in June and July, led to a split, with the moderates leaving to form a separate Feuillant Club. Only 72 of the Jacobin clubs supported this breakaway faction, but they had twice the number of deputies.

The outbreak of war with Austria in April 1792 led, once again, to the Jacobin Club splitting into two opposing factions, which was soon apparent in the new

National Convention elected in September 1792. Though there were no formal parties in the Convention, there were clear divisions between deputies of the right, centre and left. The centre majority, known as the Plain or Marais (because they occupied the lower, central seats in the Convention) were mainly uncommitted, but there were increasingly sharp divisions between the Girondins (previously known as Brissotins) on the right and the Montagnards or Mountain (those who sat in the upper seats) on the left – these last two groups both belonging to the Jacobin Club. At first, most provincial Jacobin clubs supported the Girondins, but the Montagnards dominated in Paris, and by November 1792 had won control of the Club. After a year of political struggle, the Montagnards, urged on and supported by the revolutionary crowds, seized power and ousted the Girondins in early June 1793.

The best-known Jacobin revolutionary leader was undoubtedly Maximilien Robespierre – the only one (apart from Napoleon) around whom a cult developed. The most determined leader of the Montagnards, he later came to symbolise the Terror (see pp. 60–61). Other Montagnard leaders included the young Louis Antoine Saint-Just and Georges Couthon.

The Girondins were led by Jacques Pierre Brissot, Jean-Marie Roland and Pierre Vergniaud; while Antoine Barnave, Adrien Duport and Alexandre Lameth led the Feuillants. However, as the last two groups were quickly eclipsed in the years after 1792, their leaders are little more than names.

More radical than the Jacobins was the Cordeliers Club, founded in April 1790. It had no membership fee and hence had more sans-culottes members; it was also much more in touch with the demands of the poorer classes. During the winter of 1790–91, many more popular or fraternal societies were set up in all the districts and *sections* (electoral units) of Paris, and in some provincial towns, leading to the formation of a federation of the Cordeliers and the popular societies, with an elected central committee.

Of the Cordeliers Club leaders, the most famous was Georges Danton; associated with him were Philippe Fabre d'Églantine, Jacques René Hébert (for a time), Jean-Paul Marat, and Camille Desmoulins. Though more radical on several issues than the Montagnards, their leaders and members too were mainly middle class.

Also worthy of mention, but much more loosely organised, were the political groupings known as the *Enragés* (the Angry Ones) and the Hébertists. Closely associated with the Cordeliers Club in the beginning, they soon developed a strong following in the poorest sections of Paris, and amongst the most militant of the sans-culottes. Unlike the other political groups, these had very few middle-class members and, as a consequence, became the most revolutionary of all the groups. They were often in conflict with the revolutionary governments – whether the Girondins or the much more radical Montagnards.

Of the *Enragés*, the main leaders were Jacques Roux, Jean-François Varlet, and Théophile Leclerc; while Jacques René Hébert led the Hébertists. All of these had begun as members or supporters of the Cordeliers Club, before becoming more militant oppositionists.

Crowds

The crowds which, at times, played an important and often independent role during the years 1789–95 were usually socially very mixed, consisting mainly of the more 'respectable' sans-culottes (small employers and wine merchants, shopkeepers, journalists, clerks and junior civil servants) and sections of the working classes (carpenters, stonemasons, shoemakers, tailors, builders and metal workers). The sans-culottes could be identified, not just by their wearing of trousers instead of knee breeches, but by their large moustaches, bushy sideburns and long hair, and by the revolutionary rosettes and liberty caps they wore. Occasionally, the crowds also included unskilled labourers and, as we shall see in Chapter 8, women. Very often the lead was taken by the sans-culottes – at times in alliance with the leaders of various revolutionary groupings, at times independently. Absorbing Jacobin propaganda about Rousseau's concept of direct democracy, they came to see the people as the true basis of government. Deputies were thus seen as delegates of the people – with the latter having the right to remove governments by force. Such crowds were especially influential because, for some time, they were able to control the Commune of Paris and the 48 *section* assemblies – in fact, it can be claimed that no revolutionary grouping was able to rule during the period August 1792 to July 1794 without the support of the revolutionary crowds of Paris.

There are several examples where the independent revolutionary activities of the crowds forced the pace and direction of events beyond those desired by those apparently in control. Some of these examples are discussed below.

Fall of the Bastille, July 1789

The sensational capture of the Bastille, which helped push events from political crisis to revolution, was an essentially unplanned event, with groups of people beginning to mobilise in a number of different places. Though for the two days previously there had been various parades and public meetings, organised by revolutionary leaders, the actual capture can be seen as the first of several genuinely popular or grassroots revolutionary *journées* (actions).

Capture of the Tuileries, August 1792

This revolutionary *journeé*, which resulted in the establishment of a new, more radical Commune, and the overthrow of the monarchy, is one of the earliest examples of revolutionary leaders and groups being pushed aside by popular action they themselves had instigated and attempted to manipulate. When Louis XVI had dismissed the Girondin ministers, in June 1792, their supporters amongst the sans-culottes had demonstrated with weapons in front of the Assembly and had broken into the Tuileries palace. Middle-class control of events was further weakened in July, when 'passive' citizens were allowed into the *section* assemblies and the National Guard.

Though reinstated, the Girondins quickly fell from favour with the *sections* and political clubs of Paris – their continued support for the monarchy (especially after the Duke of Brunswick's Manifesto of 1 August) led to the *journeé* of 10 August, and to the largely undirected September Massacres (see p. 60). From then on, Robespierre and the Montagnards who – much later than the Cordeliers Club, and the *sections* and Commune of Paris – decided to support a republic, began to form their own alliance with the even more revolutionary crowds, and soon came to eclipse the Girondins.

Overthrow of the Girondins, June 1793

By the summer of 1793, the crowds had become used to exerting their independent influence on the course of events, as witnessed by the activities of the *Enragés* during the food crises of February 1792 and February 1793 – especially their demand for price controls. Robespierre neither organised their actions nor supported their demands. After the September Massacres of 1792, the Girondins had attempted to limit the independence of the *sections* and the Commune of Paris. This pushed the sans-culottes into the arms of Robespierre and his supporters – but, at the same time, the Montagnards themselves gave in to the grassroots pressure for a republic. When the Girondins decided to arrest *Enragés* leaders such as Varlet and Hébert, the sans-culottes rose in an insurrection beginning on 27 May 1793. For four days, they seemed in control of Paris – the scale of the insurrection took the Montagnards temporarily by surprise, and Robespierre was initially reluctant to support their economic demands and their call for the creation of a popular *armée révolutionnaire*. Finally, on 2 June, partly in an attempt to curb the more radical demands of the crowds, the Montagnards decided to agree to the overthrow of the Girondins. Thus, sans-culotte support enabled the Montagnards to triumph, despite being weaker than the Girondins in the country as a whole. Significantly, however, the new constitution included the right to work and the right of popular insurrection.

Crisis of July–September 1793

The military defeats, counter-revolution and treason of this period resulted in the Montagnards making a new alliance with the militant sans-culottes, in order to save France from collapse. However, Robespierre was forced to make unwelcome concessions: following another insurrection in September, price controls via the Law of General Maximum were finally imposed on 39 basic items, along with the beginning of organised terror. By September 1793, it was quite clear that the revolution had been knocked off the course intended for it by the liberal middle-class leaders of the period 1789–91. Sans-culotte pressure also led to two radical members of the Cordeliers Club – Jean Marie Collot d'Herbois and Jean-Nicolas Billaud-Varenne – being added to the new Committee of Public Safety.

Thermidor, July 1794

The real significance of the sans-culottes and the revolutionary crowds was shown after Robespierre and the Montagnards, alarmed by growing radical pressure from below, united with the moderates in the Convention to reassert government control. Though Robespierre was able to have the Hébertists and the Dantonists arrested and executed in March and April 1794, these groups had many supporters in the popular societies, and in the Commune and *armée révolutionnaire* of Paris. Robespierre used tremendous propaganda in order to justify these purges, yet was very nervous about popular reaction.

Though he was able to carry through his measures, purging the Commune and disbanding the Parisian *armée révolutionnaire*, this clamp-down undermined popular support for the Jacobins. So, when Robespierre's opponents struck in late July (early Thermidor according to the revolutionary calendar adopted in September 1793), there was little popular opposition – proving, once again, that to control Paris all political groups needed the support of the sans-culottes. Though they tried to reassert themselves against the Thermidorians (the conservatives and moderates who had overthrown Robespierre) in the Germinal and Prairial risings, these were suppressed – by then, the cowed and dis-illusioned sans-culottes were no longer a significant and independent political force. François (Gracchus) Babeuf's Conspiracy of the Equals in 1796 met with little response, and was easily dealt with. The French Revolution at last resumed its original middle-class course.

The 1848 revolutions

Parties and leaders

During the period 1792–94, the lower social classes had mobilised independently and for a time had pushed the French Revolution in radical non-bourgeois directions. In all subsequent revolutions, middle-class radicals would always be looking over their shoulders, fearful that their own political struggles would bring forth successors to men such as Roux, Hébert and Babeuf – the revolutions of 1848 amply illustrate this.

As with the French Revolution of 1789, there were still no real parties in any modern sense of the term, while the leadership of the revolutionary movements of 1848 came, almost without exception, from the ranks of the liberal middle classes.

In France, the liberal opposition – including many of the more radical elements involved in the Banquet Campaign of 1846–48 – wanted electoral reform and the dismissal of Guizot. Their main leaders in the early stages were Odilon Barrot and Adolphe Thiers. In the Habsburg Empire and the German states, too, it was middle-class liberal and nationalist reformers who were responsible for the early stages of their 1848 revolutions, with leaders such as Alexander Bach and Alfred Lohner in Vienna, and Friedrich Hecker and Gustav Struve in Germany. In Italy, the early liberal and nationalist reform movement was led by middle-class individuals such as Giuseppe Mazzini, Vincenzo Gioberti, Massino d'Azeglio and Daniele Manin.

However, as well as these middle-class leaders and movements, with their liberal and nationalist demands, other more radical movements were also emerging at the same time. As we have already seen in Chapter 2, industrial development in the nineteenth century – especially in the main urban centres of western Europe – was resulting in the creation of a working class much bigger than had existed in 1789. Along with this growth, there was rising discontent amongst many of the traditional artisans and the new factory workers.

A significant proportion of these lower classes was becoming attracted to the politics of radical democracy and socialism, and they tended to follow their own leaders rather than middle-class liberals. In France, there were Albert Martin and Louis Blanc (later to be a minister in the new provisional government); and also Auguste Blanqui, who formed the far-left Central Republican Society. While in the German states, there were Stefan Born (a communist printer) and Alexander Held, as well as working-class organisations such as the *Rheberger* (for the unemployed), the *Handwerker*, and Born's *Arbeiterverbrüderung* (the first nationally based workers' organisation). While in Cologne, the Communist League had its headquarters. As the revolution unfolded, these groups were able to organise their own Artisans' Congress, which drew up their own industrial code, in general opposed to a market economy. In Italy, too – and especially in Rome – the working classes tended to form their own political clubs.

Crowds

Initially, however, the revolution of 1848 saw considerable unity and joint action between the middle-class liberal reformers and the lower classes. In fact, in most cases it is clear that rulers made concessions precisely because of this mass united opposition. Yet within a very short space of time, this unity began to unravel, as the different opposition elements started to separate out from each other, and to push for their own, often contradictory, interests.

In general, middle-class liberals were satisfied once electoral and constitutional reforms had been granted, but the lower classes continued to agitate for radical economic and social changes. It was this growing independence on the part of the workers that led many liberals to fear a repetition of the revolutionary events of 1792–94. Consequently, in an attempt to reassert control, many reformers felt forced to turn to the more conservative traditional authorities.

France

It was here that working-class independence from middle-class control was most clearly seen. The liberal reformers had not intended to overthrow Louis Philippe's regime but it was the mass involvement of the discontented lower orders (the so-called 'dangerous classes') in building, and fighting on, the barricades which had brought about the February Revolution. The middle classes were almost as shocked by events as the king and his ministers, and the situation continued to run away from them, despite the inclusion of the mechanic Albert (his surname, Martin, was rarely used) and Louis Blanc in the provisional government. Even the National Workshops Scheme (a limited public works scheme to help relieve unemployment) failed to satisfy the lower orders for long, and the number of political clubs espousing socialism and radical republicanism mushroomed. The victory of conservatives in the April elections resulted in a small insurrection in May, and in the much more serious June Days uprising, which showed in sharp relief the great gap between the two sides.

Habsburg Empire

In Vienna, the radical students of the Academic Legion had made a conscious effort to mobilise artisans and workers behind liberal demands. But the latters' growing independence and, especially, their involvement in the October Days uprising – as in France – frightened liberal reformers into retreat, allowing Windischgrätz to recapture the city. Similar artisans' and workers' unrest in Prague eventually produced the same result, as middle-class reformers moved rapidly to the right in order to reassert control and order over an increasingly independent movement.

German states

Here, too, social and economic discontent led to the artisans and workers of Berlin playing a leading role in the street fighting of the March uprising. Their support of middle-class reforms led to early concessions; but growing polarisation between middle-class and working-class interests led to the break-up of revolutionary unity.

Italian states

It was in the main cities such as Rome and Venice (where the gap between rich and poor was greatest) that many craftsmen and workers fought for a social revolution, as well as liberal and nationalist reforms. In Venice, it was the workers in the arsenal who sparked the revolution, though it was radical liberals such as Manin who took control. Soon, however, these liberal reformers became frightened by the social and economic demands of their allies. As unity began to disintegrate, many middle-class constitutionalists came to see the protection of property and the maintenance of public order as more important than continued resistance to the Austrian counter-revolution.

All in all, this general breakdown of revolutionary unity was as important a factor in the rapid collapse of the 1848 revolutions as was government recovery after initial panic. While there were strong links between liberal reformers and the popular movements, the revolutions maintained their gains. As soon as the lower orders began to initiate independent mass actions and demands, the alarmed middle classes backed off, and allowed the old authorities to reassert themselves.

The Paris Commune, 1871

Parties and leaders

In 1871, as in 1789 and 1848, there were no national parties with clearly differentiated memberships, coherent political programmes, and formal unity and discipline. The haste with which the February elections for a new National Assembly took place, and the fact that the Prussians occupied areas of France, meant there was no real opportunity for political groups to conduct any concerted campaigns in the country as a whole. However, in Paris, it was easier for political activity to take place. There, the activists of 1848 tended to come out ahead in the elections – although more extreme revolutionaries, such as Auguste Blanqui, proved to be far less popular.

During and immediately after the Prussians' siege of Paris, activists had organised many political clubs, such as the Communal Club; these then formed an all-city federation. They also established a Republican Federation and a central committee of 60 for the Parisian National Guard.

After 18 March, when the Commune rising began, it was clear that the revolutionaries were divided into loose coalitions of Jacobins, Blanquists, Proudhon federalists and Marxists (or supporters of the First International). However, it is important to realise that 21 non-revolutionaries were also elected to the new 92-strong Commune on 26 March; the overall leader was Jules Vallés. Though there were attempts to form similar *communes* in Lyons, Marseilles, Toulouse, Narbonne, Saint-Etienne, Le Creusol and Limoges, these were all quickly crushed – thus preventing the formation of a national federation of *communes*.

Crowds

Though Paris – and especially its eastern surburbs – was strongly socialist, the February elections showed starkly how unrepresentative Paris was of the rest of France. The new National Assembly was heavily conservative or monarchist, and, in Paris itself, only a small proportion of the population was actively involved in the political clubs, or in establishing and running the new revolutionary Commune. Nonetheless, it is clear that the vast majority of the people remaining in Paris – most of the wealthy had left before, during or immediately after the siege – tended to support the actions of the Commune. Hence, unlike the situations in the French Revolution and the revolutions of 1848, there is little evidence of militant crowds wishing to go in more radical directions than the ruling authority.

However, this is only true if the ruling authority is seen as the revolutionary Commune. As far as the new national government, headed by Thiers, and the new National Assembly were concerned, the people of Paris were a 'mob', a 'vile rabble and multitude' and part of a 'new invasion of barbarians', more dangerous than the Prussian troops on French soil. Hence the brutal suppression which eventually followed. Yet this was not the view of most Parisians, who had suffered greatly during the siege. It is this which explains the spontaneous action of crowds from the poorest districts in preventing the Versailles government from removing the city's cannons on 18 March. It was also a spontaneous and independent decision to execute the two generals captured that day.

Though about two-thirds of Commune members were middle class, about one-third were manual workers, and the *communard* insurrection was largely a working-class phenomenon. Over three-quarters of those arrested after the suppression were craftsmen and manual workers – with many acting as NCOs and officers in the Parisian National Guard. It was this which, rightly or wrongly, led Thiers and his government to see the Commune as the beginning of a proletarian, Marxist-influenced social revolution.

The Russian Revolution, 1917

Parties and leaders

This was the first revolution in which political parties in the modern sense really existed. Though there were several separate and well-organised political parties, including the Social Revolutionaries (SRs) and the Mensheviks, it is the Bolshevik Party that will be examined in detail here, given its crucial role in events after the March revolution of 1917.

Though Vladimir Illyich Ulyanov, also known as Lenin, was clearly the most important of the Bolshevik leaders, it is important to bear in mind that its other leaders were powerful and independent thinkers and activists in their own right. These included Grigori Zinoviev, Lev Kamenev and Nikolai Bukharin and, after August 1917, Leon Trotsky. The image which Josef Stalin and his successors (up to Mikhail Gorbachev) attempted to create – of a party always faithfully following Lenin – was totally false. On the contrary, from its foundation in 1903, through the revolutions of 1917, and at least until 1921, the Bolshevik Party had a life of its own and was riven by serious disputes over policy and action, with Lenin very often being in a minority position. In particular, the democratic element in democratic centralism – an important part of Bolshevik organisation – allowed for vigorous internal debate, and even the formation of open factions. The Bolsheviks were thus far from being a one-man band.

There are many examples of such disputes. Some of the more important ones reached down to the lower ranks of the party, which grew so rapidly during 1917 that, by December, there were over 350,000 members. Despite the fact that Lenin was absent for much of 1917 – from January to April, and from July to October – the party was more than capable of acting efficiently without him. Some of the more important inner-party disputes, which show the independence of its members, are outlined below.

April Theses

By the time Lenin returned from exile in Switzerland, in April 1917, the Bolsheviks in Russia had been giving critical support to the new provisional government for a month, despite its policy of continued involvement in the First World War. However, as soon as he returned, Lenin drafted his April Theses, calling for an end to the war, and for all power to be transferred to the soviets. As the Bolsheviks were greatly outnumbered by the SRs and the Mensheviks in the soviets, the other leaders opposed him. Only after much argument, and the calling of a special party conference, was Lenin able to get his ideas accepted.

November Revolution

From the moment that the Bolsheviks won majority positions in the soviets of Petrograd, Moscow and other major urban centres, Lenin began arguing for the Bolsheviks to overthrow Kerensky's provisional government. Yet many of the other leaders, remembering how the July Days' demonstrations had nearly destroyed their party, were reluctant; while Lenin, still a wanted man and therefore in hiding in Finland, was unable to exert any continued pressure. Two leaders – Zinoviev and Kamenev – remained totally opposed and, even after the central committee had voted 10 to 2 in favour of insurrection, in October 1917, they maintained their opposition by making public their criticisms. Even after the decision had been taken, the actual timing was decided by Trotsky, who wanted it to coincide with the Second All-Russian Congress of Soviets. Lenin on the other hand, had wanted it to take place immediately, in case another general (like Kornilov, in August) attempted a second military coup.

Coalition dispute

Immediately after the November Revolution, many Bolsheviks favoured the formation of a broad-left coalition, which was demanded by many members of the All-Russian Congress of Soviets. Prominent in arguing for such a coalition was Kamenev, and the amount of support within the Bolshevik central committee for this proposal led Lenin (who opposed it) to threaten to resign. Initially, Lenin won the vote, especially when it became clear that the other parties insisted that Lenin and Trotsky be excluded from such a government. However, Kamenev, and four others (Zinoviev, Aleksei Rykov, Pavel Milyutin and Viktor Nogin) – who had been prepared to agree to the exclusions – then resigned; three of them were also commissars (ministers) in the government. Unity was restored when, in December, a coalition was formed with the Left SRs, without Lenin and Trotsky having to step down.

Treaty of Brest-Litovsk

Some of the most serious inner-party disputes broke out over the treaty designed to end Russia's involvement in the First World War. The Bolshevik central committee split into three groups, with Lenin arguing for an immediate peace, no matter how severe the terms. However, the largest group was the left-wing communists, led by Bukharin. They wanted a rejection of the Germans' harsh terms and, instead, the launching of a revolutionary proletarian war against capitalism and imperialism, in order to hasten the approaching European revolution.

Between Lenin and Bukharin was Trotsky, who, for some time, tried to maintain a 'neither peace nor war' position. However, when Bukharin and the left-wing communists suggested that Lenin be arrested and replaced, and Lenin threatened to resign, Trotsky finally decided to support Lenin. In the end, the decision to sign the treaty was made by 7 votes to 4, with 4 abstentions. The four left-wing communists – Bukharin, Moses Uritsky, Andrei Bubnov and Georgii Lomov – then threatened to resign, although only Bukharin actually did so. A similar division was to occur in 1921, over the decision to replace War Communism with the New Economic Policy.

Crowds

It is clear that Lenin did not always completely control his party. Similarly, the crowds during the course of the 1917 revolutions also displayed considerable independence. Some notable examples are outlined in the rest of this section.

The March Revolution

The revolutionary pressures which created popular demonstrations demanding radical reforms arose, in large part, independently of any political party – including the Bolsheviks. Virtually all leaders and parties were taken completely by surprise. The explosion when it came was essentially spontaneous and with no recognised leaders. It showed early on that, irrespective of Bolshevik actions or propaganda, a popular revolution was rapidly developing.

The July Days

This revolutionary independence of the masses continued to be evident in the months after the March revolution. One aspect of this was the tremendous growth of rank-and-file militants wishing to join the Bolshevik Party – despite the fact that this was not planned, or even initially desired, by the party leaders themselves. There was also a wave of strikes, land seizures and the creation of revolutionary factory committees, workers' militias and soviets across Russia – many of these without any prompting from the Bolsheviks or the various anarcho-syndicalist (left-wing anarchist) political groups. Interestingly, these local leaders tended to be workers and much more radical than the socialist intelligentsia – including the Bolsheviks.

This reached a head in July 1917, in a local explosion of discontents when about 500,000 soldiers and workers decided spontaneously to launch an armed demonstration, demanding the end of the provisional government. There is no evidence to suggest it was started by the Bolsheviks – in fact, the Bolshevik central committee was divided on whether to support it. In the end, in order not to alienate potential supporters, and in an attempt to prevent an actual overthrow of the provisional government, they decided to participate. The Bolshevik view that the time was not yet ripe for such a workers' insurrection was proved right by the aftermath, which included the suppression of the Bolshevik Party itself. Yet this premature event clearly showed that popular sentiment and the crowds were well ahead of Bolshevik intentions. Thus the Bolsheviks can be seen as trying to ride a wave of revolution during the months of 1917.

Land and factory nationalisation

Though the Bolsheviks had encouraged workers and peasants to carry out revolutionary seizures before the November 1917 revolution, these had already begun to happen – and went on at a rapid pace across Russia, often with no Bolshevik participation at all. Even though the Bolsheviks, by the end of May 1917, began to be the majority in local factory committees and soviets, the workers tended to support the anarcho-syndicalist idea of workers' control and self-management of factories, rather than the Bolshevik policy of a centrally nationalised economy.

After November 1917, such land seizures and factory occupation began to cause problems for the new Bolshevik government – both immediately, and later over War Communism and the New Economic Policy. Though the Bolsheviks favoured landlords' estates becoming collective farms, the Peasants' Soviets voted for the SR policy of individual holdings. Forced once again to swim with the popular tide, the Bolsheviks sanctioned this by the Decree on Land. While in the cities, following the November Revolution, workers spontaneously seized even more factories. Relatively powerless to do otherwise in the early stages, the Bolshevik government, which initially favoured a form of state capitalism in order to stabilise the economy, formally nationalised many factories. This workers' radicalism also ended attempts by the Bolsheviks to negotiate financial and technical assistance from Western businesses. However, for every factory officially taken over, four more were then seized without government approval, in a spontaneous grassroots wave for workers' control. This was especially true in the areas outside the major cities, where central control was weaker.

The Kronstadt Rising, 1921
Support for anarcho-syndicalist groups and ideas continued after November 1917, and right through the 1918–20 civil war between Reds and Whites. Significantly, the Bolsheviks did not have a majority in the All-Russian Central Council of Trade Unions. Dissatisfaction with War Communism and its creeping bureaucracy once again produced political friction among the Bolsheviks, with the emergence of two left-wing opposition factions: the Democratic Centralists, and the Workers' Opposition, who first voiced their concerns in 1920.

However, outside the ranks of the Bolsheviks, demands were raised for greater soviet democracy and for a relaxation of War Communism controls. Finally, in March 1921, came the mass uprising in Kronstadt, which previously had been a Bolshevik stronghold. By March, however, new influxes of workers and sailors resulted in the majority supporting the more radical anarcho-syndicalist groups. It was clear that, once again, the Bolsheviks were out of step with many workers.

6 Barricades and blood: violence in revolutions

Introduction

Attempted revolutions and revolutionary transformations are commonly associated with violence to a greater or lesser degree – whether on the part of the insurgent masses and revolutionary groups, or on the part of the dominant social and economic groups and the political and military authorities. As a general rule, the amount of violence involved in any revolution depends on a number of key factors, including the following:

- the determination of the revolutionaries (the leaders and the crowds) to maintain and deepen their opposition and resistance;
- the resolve of the dominant groups to defend their institutions, positions and privileges;
- the degree of loyalty to the political authorities on the part of the police and army, and their willingness to carry out acts of repression.

In fact, in the early stages of a revolution, there is often much less violence and bloodshed if the revolutionary movements show real firmness – this can be seen in the 1848 revolutions, where, in the beginning, many governments capitulated almost without a shot being fired. More recently, this was seen in the 'velvet revolutions' which swept across Eastern Europe in 1989, where, with the exception of Romania, fundamental transformations were achieved with relatively little violence. On the other hand, hesitations and weaknesses by revolutionary movements at critical points can often encourage a more determined – and hence more bloody – response from the existing authorities.

However, as well as violence in the early stages of a revolution, later stages have often involved what is called 'revolutionary terror' – not to be confused with counter-revolutionary violence and terror, which will be examined in Chapter 9. Ever since the French Revolution of 1789 – and, especially, the period of Robespierre's rule in the years 1793–94 – the principle of terror has been part of the modern revolutionary tradition.

In particular, from 1789 onwards, revolutionary terror came to be seen by many revolutionaries as a legitimate way in which to destroy the enemies of the revolution, and to overcome obstacles to revolutionary transformation. This terror was also held to be crucial in maintaining the purity and revolutionary commitment of the revolutionaries themselves, by a kind of violent and permanent revolutionary process.

Such revolutionary terror is often justified on the grounds that the ordinary processes of law are inadequate for defending a revolution; and especially that a precise and limited use of revolutionary terror is the only way to prevent a much more bloody counter-revolution. This view was particularly common during the violent aftermaths of the 1848 revolutions and of the Paris Commune of 1871.

However, violence is not confined to that organised by revolutionary leaders and groups; the masses themselves often unleash spontaneous and irrational violence, which is frequently more vicious and bloody than organised violence. Furthermore, the upheaval of revolution can provide opportunities for the expression of blind prejudice and reactionary violence, such as the attacks on Jewish businesses in some of the 1848 revolutions.

The French Revolution, 1789

When the French Revolution is mentioned, images of violence and bloodshed are often the first to spring to mind – especially that of Robespierre and Saint-Just sending their opponents to the guillotine. Even supporters of the revolution have tended to see it as a glorious movement for liberty which lost its way and descended into the bloody nightmare of the Terror. However, it is important to remember that the period 1789–95 was not six years of uninterrupted violence, and that the worst phases of the Terror took place at times of often extreme national danger. In fact it is possible to distinguish four distinct phases, as discussed below.

July 1789 – December 1791

The early stages of the French Revolution, which successfully transformed France into a liberal constitutional monarchy, with an elected assembly having legislative powers, were relatively free of bloodshed and violence. Violence first erupted in the summer of 1789 in rural France, with unco-ordinated attacks on the property of the nobility. By the end of July, this had developed into the Great Fear. However, violent attacks and actual deaths were relatively few in number. In Paris, meanwhile, after the Réveillon Riots in April (which resulted in 25 deaths), had come the famous attack on the Bastille, on 14 July, which took place amidst fears of a royalist coup against the Assembly. There were over 30,000 troops in the Paris area and, on 11 July, Louis XVI had dismissed Necker, who was seen as a 'liberal'. Necker's replacement, Louis Auguste de Breteuil, was a known reactionary, favoured by the queen. During the seizure of the Bastille, about 125 of the attacking crowd were killed. The attackers then beheaded the governor, Bernard Jordan de Launay, his deputy and the former head of the city's government. Several of the guard were also killed.

The First Terror, August 1792 – January 1793

What pushed the occasional violence of the first phase of the revolution into more serious and organised violence was quite clearly the outbreak of war with Austria in April 1792. The crisis of war and a developing civil war not only helped cause what can be seen as a second, Jacobin revolution, but also led to the first of the revolutionary terrors. Tensions had begun to build up ever since the king's flight to Varennes in June 1791, and the Champ de Mars massacre on 17 July 1791, when about 50,000 peaceful demonstrators – gathered to sign a petition for the removal of Louis XVI – were fired on by the National Guard, resulting in over 50 deaths.

Furthermore, the outbreak of war in April 1792 brought early defeats and economic suffering, with consequent rumours of treachery. The appearance of the Brunswick Manifesto on 3 August led to increased demands for the overthrow of the monarchy, and to the attack on the Tuileries on 10 August, during which sections of the National Guard and a crowd of Parisians marched on the palace. In all, about 400 of the attackers were killed, while about 600 Swiss Guards, and several courtiers and servants were massacred by the victorious attackers – this made 10 August 1792 the most violent of the capital's revolutionary *journées* to date.

Further defeats, the Marquis de Lafayette's desertion to the Austrians, the entry of a Prussian army into France in mid-August, and the fall of the frontier fortresses of Longwy and Verdun only added to rumours about plots and betrayal. One result was what became known as the September Massacres, which began on 2 September in the crowded prisons of Paris holding numerous counter-revolutionary suspects. The September Massacres lasted five days, during which about 1,200 out of the total of 2,600 prisoners lost their lives. Many were hacked to death; at least half those killed were not nobles, priests or counter-revolutionaries but merely common criminals – including many prostitutes.

Though the First Terror was ended by the victories of Valmy and Jemappes, one result of the war was the trial of Louis XVI, and his execution on 21 January 1793.

The Second Terror, June 1793 – January 1794

After successes against the Prussians and Austrians in 1792, in February 1793 the Convention declared war on Britain and Holland, and then on Spain in the following month. Early defeats, the desertion of Charles François Dumouriez, and the rising in the Vendée combined, once again, to greatly increase political tensions. Emergency measures were taken from March to May 1793 to cope with the new crisis. These included the establishment of a Revolutionary Tribunal in Paris in March; the use of *représentants en mission* (members of the Convention sent to the provinces and armies to strengthen administration) and *comités de surveillance* (watch or 'police' committees in the *sections* of Paris); and the setting up of a Committee of Public Safety in April.

However, though these emergency measures were at first intended only to deal with the rising in the Vendée, they became general and permanent after the loss of Lyons. As a result, the Girondins were overthrown in June, and a new Committee of Public Safety was formed. Further federalist revolts, continued defeats, the assassination of Jean-Paul Marat on 13 July, and the discovery of Rougeville's plot to rescue the queen, culminated in the Law of Suspects of 17 September. This law gave a clearer definition of suspected counter-revolutionaries ('suspects'), allowed for their arrest by revolutionary committees, and speeded up their appearance before the Revolutionary Tribunal. This paved the way for the Second Terror which, at least in Paris, was kept in bounds by the Committee of General Security, which supervised the Revolutionary Tribunal. In Paris, it is estimated that about 2,600 were executed over a period of six months.

The story outside of Paris was much bloodier, especially where *représentants en mission* and the *armées révolutionnaires* took charge. The most notorious examples of terror were those carried out by Joseph Fouché in Lyons, Jean-Baptiste Carrier in Nantes and Paul Barras in Toulon. These were, however, the exception rather than the rule. Official executions in the countryside amounted to about 15,000, but many more were executed without trial, or died in prison.

This Terror was followed by trials and executions of the queen and the Girondin leaders in the autumn of 1793. By the winter of that year, the extraordinary dangers that had been facing the republic once more passed away, and the Terror declined after January 1794.

The Third Terror, June–July 1794

There were signs, by the winter of 1793, that even Robespierre was beginning to wish to limit the Terror or, at least, to bring the local Revolutionary Tribunals and *représentants en mission* under central control. The first major step in this process was the law of 4 December 1793 (the law of 14 Frimaire), which also abolished all the *armées révolutionnaires* outside Paris. However, opposition from the sans-culottes, increasingly over economic issues, led to an increase in popularity of Hébert and his followers. By February 1794, it appears that Robespierre had come to see the Hébertists and the Dantonists as threats to the revolution. When, in March 1794, Hébert openly called for a new revolution, Robespierre struck: Hébert and 18 others were arrested, and guillotined on 24 March. Danton and his followers shared the same fate in early April.

In May, all provincial Revolutionary Tribunals were abolished, while the law of 22 Prairial, on 10 June 1794, reduced the 'trial' times of the Revolutionary Tribunal in Paris in order to hasten executions. So began the Third, or Great, Terror, in which about 1,300 people were executed between June and July 1794. However, on 27 July (9 Thermidor) these excesses brought about Robespierre's own fall. On 28 July, he and 21 supporters were executed. After about 100 more had followed him, the last Terror came to an end.

The 1848 revolutions

The revolutions of 1848 – collectively known as the 'Springtime of Peoples' – was the biggest wave of revolutionary unrest seen in Europe since the French Revolution of 1789. Indeed, the spread of revolution in 1848 was even global, affecting countries as far away as Brazil and Colombia. In the main, the 1848 revolutions took the form of massive anti-government protest demonstrations (and occasionally riots) in major cities throughout Europe. Particularly affected were cities such as Paris, Vienna, Berlin, Prague, Budapest and Milan.

However, unlike the course of the French Revolution of 1789–95, most regimes capitulated very quickly, so the lack of any determined opposition in the early stages meant there was little serious bloodshed. Furthermore, in the brief time the revolutions appeared to be controlling events, there were no wars or invasions – this lack of external dangers meant the 1848 revolutionaries had no reason to resort to any revolutionary terror.

France

In France, the revolution really began on 22 February 1848, following Guizot's ban on a protest banquet in Paris called by radicals who had been angered by his government's refusal to extend the franchise.

A protest demonstration gathered and, although King Louis Philippe dismissed Guizot, the demonstration continued to grow. Eventually, the nerves of the troops broke, and shots were fired. The effect of this, however, was to turn protest into riot and then revolution. The following morning, over 1,500 barricades were hastily constructed across the city, and riots and disorder became widespread during the next few days. These became much more serious when sections of the National Guard handed their weapons over to the protesters. On 24 February, armed protesters even invaded the Chamber. At the same time, unrest flared up in Lyons and elsewhere. Rather than resort to more severe methods of repression, Louis Philippe abdicated and France became a republic once again. In all, about 370 demonstrators lost their lives, with no deaths amongst the police or soldiers. This relatively bloodless revolution was followed by a further crisis, in June, after a new Constituent Assembly had decided, at the end of May, to end the National Workshops Scheme. The subsequent rising, known as the June Days, saw barricades once more erected by the radicals of Paris. This was a more bloody affair, with about 500 insurgents, and about 1,000 of those involved in the government's initial repression, dying in three days of bitter fighting. The aftermath, however, was to be even more costly in terms of human life.

Habsburg Empire

Following the February 1848 revolution in France, revolutionary protests and demonstrations broke out in March 1848 in Vienna, and then in Prague and Budapest. In Vienna, demonstrations in favour of a liberal constitution attracted the support of radical students and discontented workers, and reached a crescendo on 12 March. The following day, following clashes with troops and the invasion of the Diet by demonstrators, Metternich was forced to resign. On 14 March, after no significant violence, the government appeared to have conceded many of the opposition's demands for reform. Further, small-scale violence was to occur during the October Days, in a limited rising by demonstrating students of the Academic Legion, mutinous soldiers and many workers. During this time, Count Latour was lynched by some of the protesters.

In Prague, there was similar unrest. Events in Budapest, however, were much more dramatic. There, the size of the demonstrations – at times, the crowds were as numerous as 25,000 – unnerved the authorities. In particular, they felt it unwise to use the garrison's troops, who were mostly from Italy and were not considered reliable. So, once again, an apparently easy and virtually bloodless revolution had succeeded.

German states

Apart from some limited clashes in Bavaria and some of the other states, the most dramatic events were seen in Berlin, the capital of Prussia. The events there, known as the March Days, began on 18 March, when news of Metternich's resignation reached the city. Meetings and demonstrations soon led to clashes between protesters and troops, which led Frederick William IV to promise some reforms. However, a celebratory crowd, grouped in the palace courtyard, was fired on by some panicky troops. Radical students, and discontented artisans and workers, quickly gathered in large numbers and began to erect barricades. In the four days of fighting which followed, some 300 people – mostly protesting workers and the urban poor – lost their lives. This bloodshed was enough to persuade the king to withdraw the troops, and to allow the crowds to arm themselves. Then, on 29 March, he appointed some liberal ministers. Once again, limited violence seemed to have won an easy revolution.

Italian states

The most serious fighting in the early stages of the 1848 revolutions on the Italian peninsula was seen in Milan. There, students and other young people had begun a campaign of protest in January. This turned into an open revolution on 18 March, when news reached them of Metternich's fall in Vienna. There followed five days of bitter street fighting – known as the *Cinque giornate* – between a civilian revolutionary militia and one of the best-trained armies in Europe. Then, on 22 March, Count Joseph Radetzky, the commander of the garrison, decided to withdraw his troops to the fortresses known as the Quadrilateral. In all, approximately 350 people died during this insurrection. As was the case in Berlin, most of these casualties were artisans and workers. At the same time, a much less violent revolution (involving only 3 deaths) appeared to have succeeded in Venice, under Daniele Manin.

The Paris Commune, 1871

In some ways, the Paris Commune arose in circumstances similar to those which brought to power the Jacobins during the French Revolution after 1792. The Commune was very much the product of the Franco-Prussian War of 1870–71, the siege of Paris, and the unexpected armistice of 28 January 1871. In particular, the *communards*, like the Jacobins before them, shared a belief that the temporary government had been guilty of capitulation and even treachery. It is important to realise that, in addition to heavy shelling by the Prussians, the people of Paris had suffered terribly from cold and hunger during the winter of 1870–71, before the siege was lifted: almost 12,000 died in December 1870, and almost 20,000 in January 1871.

The first violence, which resulted in the establishment of the Commune, came on Saturday 18 March, when soldiers were sent by Thiers to take possession of 417 cannons still held by the Parisian National Guard. The people of Paris, already angry at the harsh economic policies of the new National Assembly meeting at Versailles, responded quickly once news of the take-over spread. An angry crowd surrounded the government troops, most of whom were young and inexperienced. They soon responded to the calls of the crowd not to fire on the people; when the order to fire was given, most refused and gave up any pretence of resistance; soon, they were fraternising with the crowd.

However, two generals were arrested – the Commanding Officer, General Lecomte, and, later in the day, General Thomas, who was hated for his part in the bloody suppression following the June Days uprising in the 1848 revolution. At the same time, barricades were hastily erected all over the city. At first, there were only limited clashes with troops loyal to the government but, later in the day, an angry crowd demanded the execution of the two generals, by this time in the charge of the National Guard. Despite attempts by some officers to protect their prisoners, the crowd stormed the house where they were held and shot them. This was the first real violence in what was to become a very violent uprising.

Initially, however, peace reigned in Paris as Thiers ordered the city government to withdraw to Versailles, leaving the capital in the hands of the insurgents. Following elections on 26 March, the Paris Commune was proclaimed on 28 March. An attack in early April by three divisions of the Commune's National Guard on government troops ended in defeat and heavy losses for the National Guard. The real violence began on 21 May, when newly trained government troops attacked Paris. The week which followed became known as the *Semaine sanglante*, the Bloody Week. The fighting was vicious but, while the government forces lost fewer than 900 men, the number of *communards* killed in the fighting was much higher – accurate figures are impossible because of what happened after the fighting ended on 28 May.

One brutal aspect of the Commune which did much to turn people against it was the execution of about 70 of the 300 hostages held by the *communards*. Though these killings were mainly done by crowds who refused to obey orders, the fact that the Archbishop of Paris and several Dominican monks were amongst those killed was seen as particularly shocking. The desire for revenge against the rich and powerful is often manifested at some point in a revolution.

The Russian Revolution, 1917

The Russian Revolution of 1917 presents, in many ways, a sequence of events similar to that of the French Revolution of 1789: a relatively bloodless early stage leading up to the revolution; and then a more violent phase after the seizure of power, in the context of acute military threats to the new revolutionary regime. The Russian Revolution – or, more accurately, Revolutions – of 1917, like other revolutions, covered several years of unrest, with many individual acts of violence. However, six main periods of violence can be identified, as outlined below.

March Revolution

This first revolution of 1917 centred on Petrograd and was to a large extent spontaneous, with any leadership being largely the work of SRs and Mensheviks. This was partly because there were hardly any Bolshevik leaders present, either in Petrograd itself or in Russia as a whole, before March 1917.

The first major unrest began on 8 March, which saw the women of Petrograd mark International Women's Day with large demonstrations. As the workers in Petrograd went on strike in the ensuing days, several violent clashes took place between mounted police and demonstrators. Serious rioting in Znamensky Square on 11 March left 40 or more demonstrators dead after troops of the Volynsky regiment opened fire. However, this led to the first of several mutinies. As the demonstrations and clashes continued to increase in both number and size, with soldiers either joining the crowds or giving them their weapons, the authorities finally lost control of the city on 12 March. This first revolution was far from bloodless: current estimates suggest something approaching 1,500 deaths and many more wounded, as the revolutionary crowds gradually took control of the streets.

July Days

This refers to the four days, from 16 to 19 July, during which soldiers and sailors from various regiments, along with many factory workers, organised anti-government demonstrations, demanding the transfer of power to the soviets. Though this had been a Bolshevik slogan since Lenin's April Theses, it appears that these demonstrations were begun by about 20,000 soldiers from machine-gun regiments, and that the Bolsheviks only participated in them once they had begun, in an attempt to keep them peaceful. Initially, this was successful – Trotsky, for instance, prevented a crowd from lynching Victor Chernov, the minister of agriculture in the provisional government. However, violence broke out towards the end, when some government troops fired on the demonstrators who, at times, numbered as many as 500,000. The situation was confused, and this allowed the government to crush the demonstrations. In all, about 50 people, mostly demonstrators, lost their lives. Though the action was not organised by the Bolsheviks, they were blamed for it, and their party was banned.

November Revolution

Despite the myths which later surrounded the Bolshevik take-over, this really was an almost bloodless anti-climax. In Petrograd itself, there was in reality a power vacuum, as Kerensky's government by then had virtually no support at all. There was thus little serious resistance and, in all, the estimates of deaths vary between 5 and 7 – and these were mostly of insurgents rather than of supporters of the provisional government. Later on, however, there was more determined resistance in Moscow.

Civil war

It was after the Bolsheviks were in power that the revolution became much more violent. Though they were keenly aware of the events of the French Revolution of 1789, in the early days after November 1917 there was much idealism. One of the first acts of the Congress of Soviets, despite misgivings on the part of Lenin, was to abolish the death penalty – opposition to the death penalty had become part of the revolutionary tradition. However, this did not mean opposition to all violence. In fact, assassination and even limited terror were also part of the tradition of all revolutionary parties in Russia (for example, the SRs used assassination as a political weapon).

The first significant step on the road to the Bolsheviks' Red Terror was the creation of the Cheka on 20 December 1917, under the leadership of Felix Dzerzhinsky, to combat counter-revolution and sabotage. Once the civil war had begun in 1918, the Cheka began its first summary executions: official figures put the total at over 6,000 for that year, but this was probably an underestimate. A particular turning point was the resignation of the Left Social Revolutionaries from the government, and their return to assassinations – especially in August, when the Bolshevik Moses Uritsky was assassinated, and an attempt was made on Lenin's life. This resulted in almost 800 executions in Petrograd alone.

Thus, with a background of civil war, foreign interventions, assassinations and, later, of famine and economic collapse, the Bolsheviks officially resorted to a Red Terror, with a conscious reference to the Jacobin Terror of 1793–94. It is worth noting, though, that there were protests within the Russian Communist Party against what they saw as breaches of 'socialist legality'. In defence of these measures at a time of extreme danger in what the Bolsheviks saw as a national and international class war, Trotsky commented: 'We shall not enter into the kingdom of socialism with white gloves on a polished floor.'

While many of the official pronouncements about the need for a Red Terror, to combat the White Terror of their various opponents, were deliberate exaggerations (such as Trotsky's threats to execute the families of ex-Tsarist generals guilty of desertion or treachery), it is clear that the Cheka was responsible for a large number of executions. Officially, the figure for the period 1918–19 was just under 8,500 for those shot without trial, but modern estimates of those shot, with or without trial, suggest almost 50,000 executions in the years 1918–21. However, given the confused nature of the civil war, it is impossible to be precise about what happened in the provinces.

Kronstadt Rising

This event, also known as the Kronstadt Rebellion, took place in March 1921, as the Russo-Polish War of 1920–21 was coming to an end. This rising, led by SRs and anarcho-syndicalists demanding a third revolution, was crushed after bitter

This Bolshevik poster, produced during the civil war, 1918–20, shows a Red Army soldier removing the cloak from Baron Wrangel, to expose the capitalist–imperialist countries behind him. Is this poster a reliable portrayal of the role of the White generals in the civil war?

fighting, with considerable loss of life on both sides. These were especially heavy on the government side, with over 10,000 soldiers of the Red Army being killed. Furthermore, following suppression of the uprising, the Cheka executed many of the rebels and their leaders who had survived the attack – some estimates put the figure as high as 200.

'The Springtime of Peoples', 1848

6.1 The rapid spread of revolution across Europe in 1848

The revolt in Palermo against Bourbon rule in Sicily in January 1848 might have been an isolated event but for the overthrow of Louis Philippe and the proclamation of the Second Republic in France on 24 February 1848. This represented a traumatic blow to the 1815 Settlement in one of Europe's most important states, and suggested that revolutionary change could apparently be achieved relatively easily. In an obvious chain reaction, popular demonstrations in Vienna forced the resignation of Metternich (13 March); the Austrian garrison in Venice was compelled to withdraw and a Venetian republic was proclaimed (17 March); an Austrian garrison was similarly expelled from Milan (18 March); and King Frederick William IV of Prussia ordered his troops to leave Berlin (19 March). Elsewhere, revolutionary and nationalist movements challenged the survival of the German States and of the Habsburg Empire.

A common pattern of events can be discerned. Massive anti regime demonstrations occurred in capital cities such as Palermo, Paris, Vienna, Buda-Pest, Venice, Milan and Berlin. Regimes capitulated because those in power were too panicked to respond effectively and because soldiers and police were unable or unwilling to clear the streets. Therefore, concessions were immediately granted: the withdrawal of troops, the appointment of new liberal governments, the granting or promising of liberal and constitutional reforms, the formation of civil militias or national guards.

Source: W. Fortescue, 'European revolt: the 1848 revolutions', in P. Catterall and R. Viren (eds.), *Europe 1815–1870*, Oxford, 1994, pp. 52–53

6.2 Demonstrations turn to revolution in France

Victor Hugo, novelist, describing the demonstrations and barricades of 23 February 1848 in Paris

The crowds which I had seen start cheerfully singing down the boulevards, at first went on their way peacefully and without resistance . . . But on the Boulevard des Capucines a body of troops, both infantry and cavalry were massed on the two pavements and across the road, guarding the Ministry of Foreign Affairs and its unpopular minister, M. Guizot. Before this impassable obstacle, the head of the popular column tried to stop and turn aside; but the irresistible pressure of the huge crowd weighed on the front ranks. At this moment a shot rang out, from which side is not known. Panic followed and then a volley. Eighty dead or wounded remained on the spot. A universal cry of horror and fury arose: Vengeance! The bodies of the victims were loaded on a cart lit with torches. The cortege moved back amidst curses at a funeral pace. And in a few hours Paris was covered with barricades.

Source: M. Almond, *Revolution: 500 years of struggle for change*, London, 1996, p. 99

6.3 Early liberal successes in the Habsburg Empire

Thus when the news of the Paris revolution reached Vienna there was already a proto-liberal opposition in existence. Further, this opposition gained in confidence when the contents of Kossuth's speech at the Diet of Pressburg became known. The speech was translated into German by a Hungarian journalist living in Vienna and quickly distributed by the Legal-Political Reading Club. The middle-class opposition now called itself the 'party of progress' and advocated the creation of a responsible government, a broader franchise, reform of the civil service, abolition of censorship, religious toleration, universal education and the formation of a citizens' militia . . . The opposition programme quickly attracted support from all quarters, including the Diet and also the students who were active in mobilising the workers.

The rapidity of the revolution's success was remarkable, as the Court quickly assented to the demands of the reformers. On 14 March the Court accepted the idea of setting up a civic guard; censorship was lifted; and the Emperor agreed to the formulation of some kind of constitution. But this latter concession, on the face of it the most important, was in fact rather limited. Thus, although Metternich had been vanquished, the achievements of the revolution in Vienna should not be overemphasised. Significantly, the new government contained representatives of the old order, including Kolowrat and Ficquelmont.

Outside the capital events were taking a more dramatic turn, especially in Hungary. After Kossuth's speech in Pressburg, and the demonstrations in Budapest which followed it, a liberal government was formed under the premiership of Lajos Batthyany. Apparently, some 20,000 demonstrators had taken to the streets in Budapest but the garrison, made up largely of Italian conscripts, was not used as it was thought to be unreliable.

Source: P. Jones, *The 1848 revolutions*, 2nd edn, London, 1991, pp. 69–70

6.4 The beginning of revolution in the Italian states

The Austrian provinces were now the only considerable part of Italy without some form of representative government. From the beginning of the year there had been great agitation in Milan. Young Milanese had started a campaign of protest against Austrian rule in the form of a boycott of tobacco, which was a state monopoly. As a patriotic gesture everyone gave up smoking. Austrian soldiers who made a point of smoking cigars provocatively in the streets were attacked by groups of Italians, and disorder spread. The general in command of the Austrian army was Radetzky, eighty-one years old in 1848, but still an accomplished general and much loved by his troops. But the old man's dealings with Milan were foolishly severe, and the news of the fall of Metternich was enough to lead to open revolution on 18 March. For the famous *Cinque Giornate* – five days of street fighting – a civilian revolutionary army grappled with one of the most highly trained armies in Europe, until Radetzky withdrew his troops, not only from the city, but back upon the traditional defensive position of the Quadrilateral – the four fortresses of Mantua, Peschiera, Legnano and Verona which guarded the entry to Austria. A leader of the revolution in Milan was one of the deeper and more intelligent speculators on the nationalist question – Carlo Cattaneo (1801–69), who personally favoured a republican and federal solution for Italy, but who for the moment hoped that an armed rising of the whole country would make possible the summoning of a central constituent assembly, which could then decide democratically on Italy's future.

On the last of the Five Days of Milan a revolution succeeded in Venice also. The leader in Venice was Daniele Manin (1804–57), a lawyer of Jewish origin who had specialized in defending legal cases of a political complexion. Manin had been imprisoned in Venice by the Austrians, and the first action of the crowd in the March Revolution was to release him. The Austrian general in Venice, more civilized than Radetzky, withdrew his army at once from the city, after only two or three people had been killed. The Venetians proclaimed a restored Republic of St. Mark with Manin as its president, and on the same day Piedmont declared war on Austria.

Source: H. Hearder, *Europe in the nineteenth century,1830–1880*, London, 1988, p. 273

6.5 The role of young people in the revolution in Prussia

V. von Ense, a German liberal, describing workers and students fighting on the barricades in Berlin, 16–18 March 1848

'Never have I seen greater courage, a more resolute contempt for death, than in those young men who were beaten down and lost beyond all hope of rescue. Well-bred students in fine clothes, men-servants, apprentices, youths, old labourers, all went to make up a single company and vied with one another in courage and endurance.'

Source: M. Almond, *Revolution: 500 years of struggle for change*, London, 1996, p. 105

Document case-study questions

1 What, according to Document 6.2, turned the street protests in Paris on 23 February 1848 into revolution?

2 From what you have read in this book and elsewhere, explain *briefly* the following references in Document 6.1: (a) Louis Philippe, (b) the 1815 Settlement.

3 How far do Documents 6.3 and 6.4 agree about the role of young people in the street fighting of the early stages of the 1848 revolutions in the Habsburg Empire?

4 Assess the reliability of Document 6.5 as historical evidence of the barricade-fighting in Berlin 16–18 March 1848.

5 How far do these *five* documents, and any other evidence known to you, explain the rapid collapse of conservative regimes across Europe in 1848?

Internationalism: revolutions across borders

Introduction

A common feature of all of the revolutions and attempted revolutions in the period 1789 to 1917 is the impact they had beyond their own frontiers. Although there had been revolutions before 1789 (the Dutch in the sixteenth century and the English in the seventeenth century), it was not until the French Revolution of the eighteenth century – especially its 1793 constitution – that the idea that it was a basic human right to resist and overthrow oppressive regimes became generalised in Europe and, indeed, beyond.

From 1789 onwards, discontented classes and would-be revolutionaries had a model for political resistance and rebellion that could be copied and used, almost anywhere, to turn general unrest and discontent into revolution. Furthermore, the French revolutionaries were the first to take conscious actions which attempted to link their revolution to all of Europe, in a single current of subversion and revolution. One consequence of 1789 was that, from the fall of the Bastille, Europeans were either inspired – or horrified – by the prospect of political upheaval and revolution. Despite the defeat of France and the fall of Napoleon, the first half of the nineteenth century experienced so many revolutions that it became known as the Age of Revolution. After a lull in the second half of the century, the First World War resulted in another revolutionary wave sweeping across Europe until the mid-1920s, with yet another phase of revolutionary upheaval in the forty years after the Second World War, though this last wave was mainly limited to Third World countries.

Especially significant in the international aspects of revolutions after 1789 was the fact that the French Revolution became more than just a revolt against specifically French problems: the demands and slogans of French revolutionaries – such as liberty, fraternity and equality – were obviously applicable to any country in any century. Indeed some of the concepts and ideologies which emerged from revolutionary France – such as democracy and socialism – were specifically developed into consciously international movements by such intellectual revolutionaries as Karl Marx. It is important, too, to realise that technological improvements in printing and communication made the rapid spread of ideas possible – not just within a country, but also well beyond its borders.

This tendency for revolution and revolutionary ideas to become international after 1789 was also noted by conservatives – hence the alliances against Jacobin France, the attempts by Metternich in the period 1815–48 to suppress all revolutionary stirrings, and attempts after 1917 to isolate, if not destroy, the revolutionary Bolshevik regime in Russia. It became increasingly obvious to revolutionaries and conservatives alike that revolution – like economic developments – was fast becoming a globally interrelated phenomenon.

The French Revolution, 1789

This first truly modern revolution was a political upheaval which, from its very beginning, spread widely beyond the borders of France. Indeed, its revolutionary ideas, concepts, language and even symbols went much further afield, with newly independent states in Latin America, the Indian subcontinent and Africa, during the nineteenth and twentieth centuries, usually adopting the tricolor, in one form or another, as their national flag.

The early years, 1789–92

Initially, European contemporaries saw the fall of the Bastille, and subsequent events till 1792, as mainly progressive developments. Even in England, early reactions were positive, with politicians such as Charles James Fox and the Duke of Dorset greeting it warmly. Most British intellectuals and artists, such as William Wordsworth, Samuel Taylor Coleridge, Robert Southey, Percy Bysshe Shelley, Robert Burns, William Blake and Tom Paine, were supportive. Many of these, including Wordsworth and Paine, actually visited revolutionary France and sent back reports. At the same time, many of the French political clubs (especially the Jacobins) began to correspond with supporters in other countries, who saw the revolution as the dawn of a new and better age, not just for France, but for the whole of Europe. Within months, revolutionary excitement and ferment spilled across the borders of France, and began to convulse several European countries.

As already noted in Chapter 4, the spread of Enlightenment ideas in Europe as a whole, before 1789, meant almost all educated and talented people saw the first acts of the French Revolution as supporting views they themselves already held. In the early stages after 1789, considerable pro-French sentiments emerged in many of the states geographically close to France – in the Low Countries, for instance, and in the German states, where most intellectuals (including Kant, Hegel and Schiller) were supportive, and where the fall of the Bastille triggered off several insurrections, for example in Trier, Mainz, Württemberg and Hamburg in the years 1789–90. Support was also present in many of the Italian states, but it was less widespread amongst the educated classes than in the German states. In Ireland, Wolfe Tone and other republicans were so inspired by the ideals of 1789 that, in 1791, they formed the Society of United Irishmen, and began their anti-British activities. Revolutionaries in France assisted these developments by publishing pamphlets and state papers for distribution throughout Europe.

One interesting development was the establishment of political clubs (sometimes disguised as 'literary' clubs) designed to make contact and show solidarity with the revolutionaries in France. In Switzerland, where the nationalist Helvetic Society supported the revolution, clubs were set up in Basel, Zurich and Bern. A few, less long-lasting, clubs also appeared in Portugal, and in Amsterdam and other major cities in the United Provinces. In England, the Society for Constitutional Information was revived in 1791, and in 1792 the Corresponding Society was set up in London. This latter organisation was unique in that it was largely run by artisans and other working people – it has, in fact, been described by some historians as the first independent political organisation of the working classes. Elsewhere, as noted above, early support came mainly from the educated middle classes, who were inspired to campaign for limited constitutional reforms in their own countries. Significantly, in most of central and eastern Europe (with the exception of Austria, Hungary and Poland), where social conditions were different, and cultural contacts with France were weaker, there was much less support for the principles and events of 1789.

Events after 1792

The impact of the revolution on other countries changed after the outbreak of the revolutionary wars and the Terror. In the early stages, support for the revolution's ideas had been spread via publications and returning visitors. In November 1792, the Convention issued a declaration to the effect that it would 'grant fraternity and aid to all peoples who wish to regain their liberty'. However, war and terror were to lose the French revolutionaries many of their original middle-class supporters. In England, for instance, only Shelley remained as a convinced adherent. Yet sizeable minorities everywhere in Europe continued to support the Jacobins. Another consequence of events after 1792 was the emergence of a vigorous conservative reaction, with writers such as Edmund Burke in England attempting to prove why all revolution was to be avoided. As a result, European society was now clearly divided into counter-revolutionary opponents (mainly, but not exclusively, the privileged and propertied classes) and 'patriot' supporters (mainly middle-class radical liberals and artisan democrats).

Nonetheless, the impact of the changes introduced in states which were invaded by France's revolutionary armies in the years 1792–94 was far from negative as regards support for its revolution. In particular, occupation by French armies briefly revived the fortunes of the minority Jacobin movements in those countries which, before 1792, had already experienced unsuccessful insurrections. This was especially true of the United Provinces, Belgium, the Rhineland states and, to a lesser extent, the Italian states. Interestingly, Robespierre and his supporters did not really approve of the French armies acting as 'armed missionaries'; during his period of power, he attempted to restrict military intervention to merely assisting revolutions that had already begun. The wars soon turned into a revolutionary struggle against the entire *ancien régime* of Europe, with 'the people' and 'democracy' storming onto the stage of European history.

Though the reforms and political systems which came with the French occupations often ended when the French armies withdrew, the ideals of 1789–91, and many of those of 1792–94, remained behind to simmer, and eventually boil over, in the next century. This was true even after 1795 when, under first the Directory and then Napoleon, France itself seemed to lose sight of those ideals. Such concepts as the sovereignty of the people, freedom of speech, and equality before the law – and reforms which included civil codes and the abolition of serfdom – survived long after Napoleon's imperial betrayal had led Ludwig von Beethoven, and many others, to feel that all had been lost.

It was precisely because the ideas of the French Revolution were still felt to be so strong throughout Europe after 1815 that Metternich attempted to establish a reactionary conservative resistance, in the forms of the Concert of Europe and the Holy Alliance. This was supposed not only to restore the *ancien régime*, but especially to suppress all the revolutionary political forces and ideas which had been released throughout Europe after 1789. The subsequent history of many European countries in the nineteenth and twentieth centuries, however, was to show that these forces and ideas had not only spread, but had taken firm root, well beyond the borders of revolutionary France in the 25 years from 1789 to 1814.

The 1848 revolutions

Of all the revolutions in the period 1789 to 1917, the 1848 revolutions had by far the widest scope – their spread was clearly international. Sweeping with remarkable speed across most of Europe, this tide of revolution was so widespread that it even had repercussions in Latin America.

Though there were individual variations in the different states affected, it seemed to liberals and conservatives alike that the spring of 1848 was going to lead to the final and relatively easy triumph of liberalism over autocracy throughout most of Europe. For many, it seemed that the ideals of 1789, which had inspired so many in so many different states in the period 1789–1814, would at last be victorious.

It was perhaps fitting, therefore, that the first major revolutionary upheaval of 1848 (though not the very first one, which took place in Sicily on 12 January 1848) occurred in France, in February. Ever since 1789, France had continued to be the cradle of revolutionary ideals and practices in Europe. Consequently, the events in France, leading to the establishment of the Second Republic, excited middle-class intellectuals all over Europe. This French Revolution of February 1848 set off a rapid chain-reaction which seemed to signal the complete collapse of the conservative anti-revolutionary settlement of 1815.

The almost immediate influence of this revolution beyond France's national frontiers was seen most dramatically in Austria, where, within 16 days of the abdication of Louis Philippe in France, the arch-conservative Metternich was forced to resign as chancellor on 13 March. This was a second, and equally important, turning point in the 1848 revolutions and, along with news of the events in France, accelerated the capitulation of many more regimes in Europe – most notably in other parts of the Habsburg Empire, and in the Italian and German states. The manner of Metternich's flight across Europe, into exile in England, seemed to many to symbolise the sweeping away of autocracy by the twin revolutionary brooms of liberalism and nationalism. The combined impact of events in Paris and Vienna was momentous: on 17 March, victorious revolutionaries declared a republic in Venice; the next day, Milan experienced a similar revolt; while on 19 March, demonstrations in Berlin led Frederick William IV to lose his nerve and grant liberal reforms, with similar moves to appease those nationalists who desired a united Germany. Elsewhere, similar events unfolded in what appeared to be a common pattern, crossing border after border in the spring of 1848.

Other areas of Europe significantly affected by this revolutionary tide of liberalism rippling across the continent included the Iberian peninsula. In the months March to May, there were two uprisings in Madrid, and smaller ones in several other towns. These, however, were unsuccessful, and were quickly suppressed. In Portugal, there was a delayed reaction – the situation remained quiet in 1848 but, in the spring of 1851, revolutionary action, based on the liberal demands of 1848, finally broke out. Strangely, the situation in the Low Countries remained mainly calm during 1848 – unlike 1789 – despite the fact that liberals and would-be revolutionaries there still tended to look to Paris and France for inspiration. Also relatively untouched were England, where the great Chartist demonstration in London in April was unsuccessful; and Russia, which had yet to experience the destabilising effects of industrialisation and urbanisation.

Thus, the political experiments made in Paris in the spring of 1848 were as much an inspiration to many liberal reformers and revolutionary democrats across Europe as were the earlier experiments between 1789 and 1794. In the same way, French examples combined with specific local strands of discontent and hope to turn much of the continent into a revolutionary ferment. The results, too, were broadly similar: deceptively early victories, apparently ushering in the dawning of a new era of freedom and fraternity, which was marked by the granting of liberal constitutions, the appointment of liberal ministers, the winning of civil liberties and, where appropriate, measures leading to national unity and/or self-determination.

Though, as we shall see, many of these liberal triumphs soon turned to defeat, one significant consequence of the February 1848 revolution in France was that, because of its wide regional appeal, the general political stability established by the conservative settlement of 1815 was irretrievably shattered. However, as indicated by the June Days uprising in Paris between 23 and 26 June – and by similar events in Vienna, Berlin and Venice – the new revolutionary spectre was to be socialism rather than liberalism. Significantly, this new political movement was to adopt an even more consciously international approach.

The Paris Commune, 1871

The Commune of 1871 was a specific response to a particular situation in France, and was isolated by the Franco-Prussian War and its aftermath. This meant that, unlike the revolutions of 1789 and 1848, it did not spread quickly or widely elsewhere – apart from two limited and abortive attempts in France itself.

Nonetheless, during its short existence of 72 days, the Paris Commune did find lots of supporters across Europe. These were drawn mainly from amongst ordinary working people – often, they were members of trade unions, and a significant minority were supporters of Marx's First International. They sent messages of support, and even organised – where possible – public meetings of solidarity. The largest such demonstration took place in Hyde Park in London, on 16 April 1871, with over 30,000 participants. In addition, despite the defeat of the Commune the following month, the *communards* were to bequeath to the international workers' movement two long-lasting symbols: the red flag of socialism, and the famous song of communism, the 'Internationale', which was written by *communard* Eugène Pottier.

However, the real international significance of the Commune was not so much its actions, as the myths and legends which soon came to surround them: these were to give it a significance far greater than it had had during its three months' existence from March to May 1871. The Commune soon came to be seen as the first revolution of the industrial age, promising a new era of social rather than political revolution. The left came to view it as the first shot in the international class war which would ultimately lead to the total victory of the working class. On the other hand, the right came to see it as the first sign of the imminent socialist revolution, which they feared was being organised by the international workers' movement. Indeed, as it coincided with the zenith of the First International's popular appeal and spread, many conservatives overestimated the role of the First International in the Commune, and saw it as already able to mastermind a universal revolution. One result was to convince Bismarck to take measures against the growing socialist movement in the new Germany.

An important explanation for these exaggerations and legends about the Commune can be found in the writings of Karl Marx. He referred to the *communards* as 'those Parisians storming heaven', and saw the Commune as 'the glorious harbinger of a new society'. He clearly saw it as the first concerted attempt by the proletariat to overthrow capitalism, and to begin the socialist transformation of society via the political lead of the working class. As Marx was the most distinguished and influential contemporary revolutionary, his exaggerated interpretation of the Commune was bound to have considerable influence on the international workers' movement, and thus transformed the Commune into one of the greatest events in its history.

Of particular importance in making the Commune of international and long-term influence was Marx's account of it in *The civil war in France*. Future revolutionaries across the world came to see the Commune as the model of how to achieve their ends. Some, however, later viewed it as the last serious attempt to repeat urban insurrection along the lines of 1789 or 1793, its disorganised idealism and rapid defeat leading to the conclusion that organised revolutionary parties were needed – in particular, to demoralise or revolutionise armies.

One future revolutionary influenced by Marx's writings on the Commune was Lenin, who based his *State and revolution* (written in 1902, while in exile) on Marx's pamphlet *The civil war in France*. After the 1917 revolution, the Bolsheviks consciously counted the days until their regime had outlived the Commune; later, Lenin was to state that 'the young Soviet Republic stood on the shoulders of the Paris Commune'. Thus Marx's interpretations and exaggerations – if not the actual facts – of the Commune were to have long-term international significance.

Yet some of the romantic but powerful myths about the Commune stem from the *communards* themselves: their Declaration of 27 March claimed they were inaugurating 'a new era of politics – experimental, positive and scientific', while their Manifesto claimed it had begun 'the end of the old world'. The Commune was seen by many as a 'festival of the oppressed', showing the world that working people could govern themselves. It thus came to inspire communists and anarchists well beyond the nineteenth century – its ideas and actions were still being studied and discussed by revolutionary students in France in May 1968.

Ultimately, the Commune was more important as a symbol and example for future revolutionaries. Though it did not seriously threaten the bourgeois status quo in 1871, it certainly frightened the economic and political elites: its very existence seemed to put flesh – and blood – on the spectre of communist revolution that Marx had threatened in the Communist Manifesto in 1848. It can thus be seen as the forerunner of the 1917 Revolution in Russia.

The Russian Revolution, 1917

The Russian Revolution of 1917, widely regarded as the most important single event of twentieth-century history, was certainly the most consciously international of all the revolutions in the period 1789–1917. Even historians unsympathetic to the Bolshevik revolution have accepted its tremendous significance: according to Richard Pipes, 'the Russian Revolution was the single most consequential event of the twentieth century, whose repercussions have been felt in every corner of the world'.

The French Revolution of 1789 had first introduced the idea of revolution as a phenomenon which defied frontiers and, following this example, future revolutionaries came to see it as their duty to help fan the flames of revolt. In 1848, less than 60 years after the fall of the Bastille, Europeans had once again seen revolution spill across borders in an epidemic of revolutionary contagion. Early on, Lenin had said: 'the social-democratic movement is international in its very essence'; and it was accepted by all Bolshevik leaders that the coming socialist revolution would follow this pattern, spreading rapidly all over Europe via a combined process of political inspiration and revolutionary assistance.

When the Bolsheviks took power in 1917, they immediately began to use the organs of state to promote the revolutions they expected to sweep across a

Europe so devastated by the First World War. To the Bolsheviks, who had always called for world revolution, it seemed inconceivable that, given the current crisis of world capitalism, the revolution would be confined to Russia. Their call for workers to smash the old order – reminiscent of the Jacobins of 1793 – seemed to be well-timed, with demonstrations supporting the Bolsheviks taking place in Berlin, Paris, and in several cities in Italy and Scotland. These early signs of revolutionary ferment caused Lenin to say: 'Bolshevism has become the world-wide theory and tactics of the international proletarian movement . . . Never have we been so near to world revolution.' In January 1918, their Declaration of the Rights of the Toiling and Exploited Peoples included reference to the right of self-determination in a bid to spread the revolution to colonies in the Third World.

From the beginning, Trotsky, as commissar for foreign affairs, saw his main function as being to assist the spread of world revolution. He immediately set up a section for propaganda, in order to produce *Die Fackel* (*The Torch*) – a revolutionary newspaper published, in various languages, for German and Austro-Hungarian prisoners of war. Even during the peace negotiations at Brest-Litovsk, permission was obtained for fraternisation, in order to help spread Bolshevik ideas and so speed a revolution in Germany. Lenin saw the Bolshevik revolution acting, like the Paris Commune of 1871, as an inspirational example and spark. He seemed to have been proved correct when, eight months later, mutinies began to erupt amongst the German army and navy.

Inspired by Bolshevik actions and ideas, a strike wave spread across the continent in the years 1917–18. In Britain in 1918, there were 1,165 strikes involving over a million workers; here, as elsewhere, strikes were very often led by unofficial and more radical militants. From 1918 to 1923, strikes and mutinies turned, in many countries, into revolution. The first, and potentially most significant, began in Germany in October 1918. A naval mutiny at Kiel soon spread to other northern ports, soviets were formed and, as unrest moved inland to include Berlin and other cities, the Kaiser fled and abdicated. A revolutionary Council of People's Representatives acted as a provisional government. This was a real relief for the Bolsheviks, as they did not believe that Russia, on its own, was advanced enough to build a new socialist society. The upheavals continued and, in January 1919, revolutionary crowds, led by Rosa Luxemburg and Karl Liebknecht and the Spartacists, declared a revolutionary soviet republic.

In Budapest, in March 1919, Béla Kun declared a Bolshevik soviet republic in Hungary, after a confused revolutionary seizure of power by communists and social democrats. The next month, revolutionary socialists and communists in Munich announced the formation of the Soviet Republic of Bavaria. In Austria, workers' and soldiers' soviets were set up, to be followed by an attempted communist rising in June 1919. Italy began to experience a wave of strikes, factory occupations and, by 1920, the establishment of soviets in Milan, Turin and various other towns, as well as in some rural areas, where peasants seized land. From 1918 to 1920, Spain saw great revolutionary socialist and anarchist unrest, in what became known as the Three Red Years (*Trienio Bolshevista*). Unrest also increased in Britain and France. In 1918 in Britain the Labour Party –

directly influenced by the Bolshevik revolution of 1917 – adopted Clause 4, which committed it to the public ownership of industry, and only narrowly voted to adopt a parliamentary as opposed to a soviet road to socialism. Significantly, there were many mutinies amongst troops sent to intervene in the Russian Civil War on the side of the Whites – for instance, in British and French regiments. At the same time, many trade unionists, sympathetic to the new workers' state, were reluctant to load or transport military supplies intended for the Whites – for example, the 'Hands off Russia' campaign in Britain.

Encouraged by what the Bolsheviks clearly saw as the imminent victory of revolutionary socialism, they optimistically set up the Third, Communist, International (Comintern) in March 1919, in order to help these revolutionary developments. Revolutionaries such as Lenin had, since 1915, been calling for such a replacement for the Second, Socialist, International, which was held to have betrayed internationalism in 1914 when, with the exception of its Russian and Italian members, the parties involved had supported their respective governments. The first Congress of Comintern took place in March 1919, in Moscow, with representatives from 41 countries. Its main decision was to call for the formation of communist parties in each country. In the years 1919–21 this call was answered all over Europe and beyond, with the Chinese Communist Party being formed in 1920. However, at the time of the formation of Comintern, the Bolsheviks were in the midst of the civil war, dealing with White armies and foreign intervention. They were thus unable to give much direct theoretical or organisational help to these revolutionary struggles from 1918 to 1920.

By the time of Comintern's second Congress, in July 1920, when the civil war in Russia was virtually over, the situation elsewhere was clearly changing. The Spartacist Rising of January 1919 had been defeated, with Luxemburg and Liebknecht murdered. The Bavarian Republic had been crushed in May and the communist rising in Vienna, in June, had been easily suppressed. In August 1919, the Hungarian Soviet collapsed, following military defeats, while revolutionary stirrings in Poland in 1920 came to nothing. Though revolutionary hopes generally remained high in 1920 with the now better-organised Comintern, which described itself as the 'fighting organ of the international proletariat', it was clear that the revolutionary tide was beginning to ebb. Though outbreaks of unrest continued during the years 1921–23, it was soon clear that – despite the fervent hopes of the Bolsheviks – Soviet Russia was going to have to survive at least for a time as an isolated revolutionary island in a hostile capitalist sea. This was a bitter setback, as Russian revolutionaries had justified their seizure of power on the socialist revolution spreading to more advanced countries, which was seen as their only hope for survival.

This totally unexpected state of affairs was to have severe repercussions on the internal history of the Soviet Union. However, Comintern continued to expand in the 1920s and 1930s, ensuring that fears of imminent socialist revolution continued to exist in Europe. If the Paris Commune of 1871 can be said to have put flesh and blood on Marx's spectre of communist revolution, the Bolshevik Revolution of 1917 and its aftermath seemed to give it world-wide life and vigour.

8 Revolutionary women

Introduction

Until recently, one of the least researched aspects of the history of revolutions has been the involvement and contributions of women – despite the fact that it involves some 50 per cent of the population at any given period. In the last 20 years, however, there have been attempts to redress this historical imbalance, albeit mainly by feminists and female historians.

In general, political and historical analysis shows that most people are politically inactive most of the time; and that women tend to be less politically aware and involved than men, whatever historical period is under consideration. However, as with men, the extraordinary circumstances associated with revolutions both impel and enable women to organise themselves. The turmoil that is revolution creates an environment in which everyone – including women – can associate and act on behalf of their own interests, and can begin to participate in public life.

In all of the revolutions examined in this book, educated women used the opportunities provided to raise radical social, economic and political demands, specifically designed to transform women's place in the family and in the economy – in particular by demanding legal rights and equality. However, women from the lower classes also participated, especially when economic problems threatened the living standards of themselves and their families. Often, such women went on to connect these issues with the power struggles and radical political changes taking place, and made full use of the opportunity to press for legal and constitutional reform. As we shall see in this chapter, collectively, women have at times played significant roles in revolutions. In some, they have even contributed to the creation of genuine turning points.

In the main, however, male revolutionaries seem to have given little consideration to the rights of women. Furthermore, women themselves have rarely gone beyond supporting, or acting through, their men. In fact, many men have apparently feared women's involvement in political activity. Consequently, male politicians and historians have often either ignored women revolutionaries or portrayed them as Amazons and furies, while even many radical men have at times seemed reluctant to support women's rights, in case they appeared foolish in the eyes of other men.

Nonetheless, since 1789, many feminists and women revolutionaries have succeeded in placing women's rights on the political agenda, and in making women's issues an increasingly important theme in nineteenth- and twentieth-century struggles and revolutions. This they have done by raising demands, and taking part in revolutionary activities, on their own account.

This chapter will examine three aspects of the role of women in revolutions: actions, organisations and activists.

The French Revolution, 1789

Actions

Collectively, women of most social classes played significant roles during the crisis points of the French Revolution outlined below.

The October Days, 1789

Although women – including those from the lower classes – were present in the crowds which stormed the Bastille on 14 July, there is no evidence to suggest they were involved in planning it. However, growing economic problems during the summer, such as high bread prices and the decline of luxury trades and services, hit women especially hard. This stimulated more active protest, including bread riots in August and September. By early September, ordinary women were beginning to act in new and untraditional ways. Market women and laundresses, in particular, were involved in processions and demonstrations almost every day.

This illustration shows the March of the Women to Versailles on 5 October 1789. What impression of the women does the cartoonist seem to be trying to convey?

Finally, on 5 October women from the central market districts and from faubourgs (suburbs) such as Saint-Antoine launched a mainly spontaneous demonstration and occupied the Hôtel de Ville, after the king and queen had welcomed royal troops into Versailles. This led to the first example of an alliance between ordinary women and the radical wing of the National Guard. The subsequent march to Versailles was essentially the result of women giving a lead to their menfolk. It ended with the royal family being forced, along with the National Assembly, to move to Paris. This women's insurrection, while making traditional female demands for stable supplies and bread prices, also took up *political* demands. These included the call for Louis XVI to accept the decrees of 4 August and the Declaration of the Rights of Man.

Taxations populaires, 1792 and 1793

From 1790 to 1791 there was relative social calm, with educated middle-class women pressing for specific legislation to improve the position of women. However, many women were very active in the lead-up to, and on the day of, the Champ de Mars mass rally and petition. On 16 July, the day before the massacre, two women proposed in the Cordeliers Club that all statues of the king be knocked down. This was rejected by the male majority. Several women were amongst those arrested after the National Guard had killed about 50 of the demonstrators.

It was the outbreak of war with Austria in 1792, and the increased economic hardships it brought, that once again pushed thousands of women into action. Often, women proved more ready than men to combine legal methods (such as petitions) with more violent means. In January and February 1792, ordinary women – mostly laundresses, market women and other workers – took petitions to the Commune and the Legislative Assembly, protesting about shortages and prices. When they were ignored, they took direct action in the form of the *taxation populaire* – popular imposition of fairer prices – mainly in the faubourgs and the central markets of Paris.

These protests of 1792, known as the Sugar Riots, eventually came to an end, but continued distress and a refusal by the authorities to take measures to protect women's interests led to the much more widespread and better-co-ordinated *taxation populaire* of February 1793. This time, there was extensive damage to property, and the National Convention agreed to consider price controls. By then the ordinary women of Paris had become a powerful political force, though all leading politicians were still male.

Germinal and Prairial, 1795

In the main, women were supporters of the early Montagnard rule in 1793 and their Law of the General Maximum (see p. 49). But growing centralisation led to disillusionment and a decline in political activity. This was greatly accentuated after Thermidor (see p. 50), which saw a concerted attempt to encourage women to return to the more traditional concerns of home and family.

However, the Thermidorian return to laissez-faire economic policies, from October to December 1794, led once again to increased hunger and want. During the winter and spring of 1795, women had to deal with shortages and long queues. This resulted in explosions of discontent in April (Germinal) and May (Prairial) – which turned out to be the last popular insurrections of the French Revolution. In March, women took the lead in raiding bakeries, initiating processions and demonstrations to the *section* assemblies and enforcing price reductions. On 20 May, women began the most stubbornly fought social protest of the whole revolution. It lasted four days, beginning with a massive invasion of the Assembly by housewives and market women. In addition to demands about supplies and prices, they also demanded the implementation of the Constitution of 1793.

Outraged, the Thermidorian regime took harsh measures to repress and humiliate the women involved. A whole generation of revolutionary women who had begun to advance women's issues was silenced – nothing that could compare with the Prairial Days would appear again until 1848.

Organisations

In the early years of the revolution, many women began to attend the various political clubs and societies that sprang up, especially the Cordeliers and Jacobin Clubs. Though these overwhelmingly male societies were prepared to tolerate women applauding their favourite speakers, shouting out comments, and drafting and presenting petitions, women were generally discouraged from taking a more active and formal part in their proceedings. Of the male revolutionists, only Condorcet and Robespierre seriously contemplated extending political rights to (propertied) women. Nonetheless, these clubs, popular societies and the elective *section* assemblies, which women could either attend or even join in some cases, were extremely important in raising women's revolutionary understanding.

By 1793, however, groups such as the *Cercle social* (established January 1790), which had begun to demand educational and political rights for women, had widened to include women sans-culottes. Particularly important were the Fraternal Society of Patriots of Both Sexes and the Friends of the Constitution, which admitted women as full members and officers. More radical women seized the opportunity to form correspondence societies, and federations of women's groups.

The most significant organisation, however, was the Society of Revolutionary Republican Women (SRRW), set up in February 1793. This was the first political interest group for ordinary women to be established in Europe. Founded by an actress and a chocolate-maker, it was linked to the left-wing *Enragés*, and fought for the interests of the working poor, with most of its members being working women. These *républicaines–révolutionnaires* supported the Montagnards in their political struggle with the Girondins, and merged the interests of middle-class radicals with those of the Parisian poor.

The SRRW had contacts in all the *sections*, and played a key role in the Montagnard take-over of 31 May – 2 June, guarding the doors of the National Convention, and refusing to admit Girondin deputies. The SRRW also pushed hard for the Montagnards to reject a market economy in favour of price controls and the regulation of supplies. Dissatisfaction led them to stop supporting the Montagnards in August, and instead to strengthen their alliance with the *Enragés*. By September, several hundred women were regularly meeting in the SRRW club in the former church of Saint-Eustache, and they decided to increase their pressure on the Montagnards. Demonstrations and petitions finally resulted in a number of successes:

- 5 September – a legal Terror was decreed;
- 9 September – an *armée révolutionnaire* was created;
- 17 September – the Law of Suspects passed (see p. 61);
- 21 September – a decree to make all women wear the revolutionary cockade (a red cap or a red ribbon worn on a cap) in public;
- 29 September – the Law of the General Maximum passed.

However, not all women were so radical – for example, the market women objected to price controls, and to the wearing of the cockade. The result was occasional street violence, and petitions against the SRRW during October. As part of the Montagnard drive for centralisation, on 30 October they declared all women's clubs and associations illegal, and the leaders of the SRRW were briefly detained. After Thermidor, women were excluded from the public galleries of clubs and from *section* assemblies and, in October 1794, all political clubs lost the right to affiliate, correspond or petition.

Activists

The best known is probably Marie-Jeanne 'Manon' Roland who, influenced by Rousseau, became a republican *philosophe* at a young age, and undoubtedly helped shape Girondin policy. She fell with them, and was executed on 9 November 1793. But many other educated women also actively participated in revolutionary politics, for example Etta Palm d'Aelders, a Dutch woman who campaigned hard for women's rights, including equal education and employment opportunities; and Olympe de Gouges, who, angry that the Declaration of the Rights of Man did not include women, drafted and presented a Declaration of the Rights of Women. Also important was Théroigne de Méricourt, who participated in the October Days of 1789, setting up the Friends of the Constitution group in 1790; she was also a strong advocate of an armed female battalion, though she failed to found a specifically women's group.

Other women, however, were impatient with these essentially bourgeois women and their groups, and instead became much more militant, actively fighting for the interests of the women sans-culottes. The most influential were Claire Lacombe (actress) and Pauline Léon (chocolate-maker), who were both founders and presidents of the SRRW. Imprisoned after their society was banned, Léon was released in August 1794, but Lacombe remained a prisoner until August 1795.

The 1848 revolutions

Actions

The activities of women during the revolutions of 1848 have only recently become a topic of serious historical research. Historians are divided over whether women played as leading a role in 1848 as they had done in 1789. However, there is general agreement that those who did participate were extremely active. Peter Stearns, for example, states that women's enthusiasm in 1848 was possibly *greater* than in 1789, with women participating vigorously during some of the revolutionary fighting. This was particularly true in the more industrialised towns and cities, where developing capitalism was involving increasing numbers of women in factories, and especially in outworking in the relatively less-skilled crafts. It was in such centres that the socialists and early communists – the only political groups supporting the idea of equality for women – were to be found.

France

It was in Paris, the centre of European revolutionary tradition and where socialist and communist ideas had their greatest influence, that the women of 1848 were able to organise the only really independent women's initiative. Women were active in the creation of trade associations and the conduct of strikes, while unemployed women successfully agitated for the National Workshops Scheme to be applied to women as well as men. There were also women's trade representatives on the Luxembourg Commission set up by Louis Blanc and the provisional government to examine and make recommendations on workers' pay and conditions.

Advocates of the rights of women also issued thousands of posters, bulletins and proclamations, as well as founding journals and newspapers, the most important of which, *La Voix des Femmes* (*The Voice of Women*), advocated divorce, and day-care centres for working women. Outside of Paris, women's efforts tended to be limited to urging their men to take action. In the radical villages of south-east France, for instance, the women sent their men to fight for 'the good cause', while they guarded the villages. However, as the politicisation process characteristic of the 1848 revolutions unfolded, women's political participation tended to increase. Some women had fought on the barricades during the February Revolution, but far more were involved in the bitter street fighting in June 1848. The women of Paris fought as fiercely as the men, and made up a small percentage of those killed, wounded or arrested. Though some restricted themselves to loading and cleaning guns, others led fighting groups consisting entirely of men. There was a clamp-down on women's political activity after the repression of the June Days uprising, but large numbers of women had had their social and political consciousness extended.

Habsburg Empire

As in France, women tended to see their political activity as mainly supportive of that of men – though their support was often considerable. Women in large cities such as Vienna and Prague often met to debate public matters, and to edit newspapers. In general, however, there is little evidence of women demanding new rights for themselves. Nonetheless some women did participate in the fighting: in Prague in June 1848; and in Vienna in October 1848, when women helped by digging up the pavements and building barricades. In Hungary, two female regiments volunteered for Lajos Kossuth's new army. Though sidelined into hospital and munitions work, several women joined the Hungarian troops disguised as men – at least two made the rank of captain before being discovered.

German states

Here, too, women's roles tended to be supportive. In Elberfeld, a textile town in western Germany, women held a public meeting on 31 March in support of workers and the unification of Germany, proposing that people could contribute to the cause by wearing only German-produced clothes. Other women began to collect for a German navy. Women also participated in mass meetings, festivals and demonstrations, though mostly only the peaceful ones. During the critical days of September 1848, some of the more left-wing women in Württemberg organised a women's petition which was intended to urge their men to take militant political action. However, in the context of a mid-nineteenth-century patriarchal society, such public political initiatives by women were an important development.

Italian states

Here, even before 1848, women were a force in public life – but only as supporters of husbands, sons or fathers and their revolutionary activities. Giuditta Sidoli, for instance, had a lifelong attachment to Mazzini, who declared publicly during the 1848 revolutions that women should enjoy full equality with men. Many Italian women were fierce nationalists and enthusiastic liberals; during the revolutions they encouraged their sons and husbands to fight, or themselves were involved in establishing hospitals for the wounded.

Organisations

One widespread feature of the 1848 revolutions was the springing up of hundreds of political clubs across Europe.

France

In February 1848 women formed the *Vésuviennes*, which, as well as raising specifically women's demands, also recruited unmarried women aged 15–30 for a year's semi-military training. Other clubs specifically for women included the Club for the Emancipation of Women and the Union of Women: members of these clubs demanded equal rights, the legalisation of divorce, and – most radical of all – the right to vote. Altogether at least six such clubs were established, after several radical clubs run by men rejected their demands. The Fraternal Association of Democrats of Both Sexes also debated and supported these issues; while many women sat in the gallery of Blanqui's Central Republican

Society. Though most clubs were based in Paris, many also appeared in smaller provincial towns, but there are no exact figures for the total number of clubs.

Habsburg Empire and Italian states
Relatively few women became involved in political clubs in these areas, though in Prague there was the Club of Slavic Women, established to promote the education of girls in their national language. In Prague and Vienna women also formed clubs and associations to assist political refugees and imprisoned insurgents. Apart from Prague and Vienna, however, there is little evidence of women meeting to debate public matters in clubs specifically set up by women.

German states
Here, too, men in general were reluctant to allow women to attend, let alone speak at or join, the many radical political clubs established in 1848. The socialists and communists, however, were much more supportive; and in Berlin, the small Workers' Congress, representing 31 different clubs, supported the call for equality for women. It was also in Berlin that women set up the Democratic Women's Club. Though it mainly dealt with social issues, it also followed political developments, and was very supportive of the socialist Alexander Held, making him the only man allowed to enter their club.

Activists

France
It was France which produced the majority of well-known women revolution-aries in 1848. Eugénie Niboyet edited the *Voice of Women*, one of several Parisian newspapers specially devoted to women's issues; while Jeanne Déroin, a seamstress, was active on the left, and founded the Club for the Emancipation of Women. When Jeanne Déroin proposed to run as the democratic candidate in the May 1849 elections, P.-J. Proudhon condemned her on the grounds that the organs women possessed to nourish the young made them unsuited for the vote – her reply was to ask him to show her the male organ that qualified him to vote! Forced to flee to England in 1851, following Louis Napoleon's coup, she remained an active feminist until she died, aged 89. Also important was Joséphine Courbois, whose heroic fighting on the barricades of Lyons earned her the title 'Queen of the Barricades'; she went on to fight in the Paris Commune of 1871. George Sand (real name Amadine Lucile Aurore Dudevant), too, had some influence on the political life of 1848. Influenced by Saint-Simon's socialism, she was an ardent republican, and a supporter of barricades and revolution. She was the best-known female intellectual of her day, and many of her 109 books reflected her humanitarian ideas. Initially associated with Armand Barbés, the radical leader of the Club of the Revolution, she soon became adviser to Alexandre Ledru-Rollin, minister of the interior in the new revolutionary government, editing the *Bulletins of the Republic*, which helped spread radical republicanism in the provinces.

German states

The best-known feminists in the German States were Mathilde Franziska Anneke and Luise Otto-Peters, who were very active, and who both edited newspapers. Anneke was especially prominent, and moved from radical to communist politics; after the failure of the 1848 revolution, she fled to the USA, where she continued to campaign for women's rights.

Italian states

In Italy, apart from Giuditta Sidoli, there was Anita Garibaldi, the one real Italian heroine of 1848, who fought at Garibaldi's side. Many Italian noblewomen were also active in supportive roles, such as Princess Belgioioso in Rome; Marchioness Constance d'Azeglio; and, in Venice, Theresa Manin, Daniele Manin's wife.

The Paris Commune, 1871

Actions

From the very beginning of the Commune, the women of Paris were active. It was, in fact, women who first raised the alarm on 18 March that government soldiers were attempting to move the city's cannons; while women were to the front in the crowds which prevented the soldiers from taking them. In particular, women worked in arms and ammunition factories, made uniforms, and staffed makeshift hospitals, as well as helping to build barricades. Many were attached to the battalions of the National Guard as *cantinières*, supplying food and drink to the soldiers on the barricades, along with basic first aid. In theory, four *cantinières* were intended for each battalion, but in practice, there were often many more. Furthermore, there is much evidence to show that many women picked up the guns of dead or wounded men, and fought with great determination and bravery. There was also a 120-strong women's battalion of the National Guard which fought bravely on the barricades during the last week of the Commune. Forced to retreat from the barricade in Place Blanche, they moved to Place Pigalle and fought until they were surrounded. Some then escaped to Boulevard Magenta, where all were killed in the final fight.

At a time when women still had few legal rights, and no vote, many saw the Commune as an opportunity for women's liberation. Many women thus involved themselves in workers' co-operatives, and even established their own trade unions. Women involved on the various committees of the Commune drew up plans for an industrial training school for girls, and for day-nurseries for working mothers.

Some sources refer to women as incendiaries – *les pétroleuses* – setting fire to public buildings during the final *Semaine sanglante* of the Commune. Such stories appear to have been government-inspired anti-feminist scaremongering, and most foreign correspondents present did not believe them. Nonetheless, hundreds of women were summarily executed – even beaten to death – by government troops who suspected them of being *pétroleuses*. Yet, despite the fact that many more women were later accused of being incendiaries, the councils of war did not find a single one guilty of that offence. However, there is evidence to suggest that, during the final days, women held out longer behind the barricades than did the men. In all, 1,051 women were indicted before the councils of war, held between August 1871 and January 1873: 8 were finally sentenced to death, 9 to hard labour, and 36 to transportation to penal colonies.

Organisations

As in previous revolutions, women – one of the most oppressed sections of society and, hence, with most to gain – quickly involved themselves in political activity. Many joined, and were very active, in mixed-sex political clubs, such as the Club of the Proletarians and the Club of Free Thinkers, ensuring that equal rights for women were discussed. Women also set up their own organisations, such as the Union of Women for the Defence of Paris and Aid to the Wounded, founded by supporters of Marx's First International. This tried to achieve equal pay for women and a reduction in working hours, and had representatives from the 20 *arrondissements* of Paris. Others included the Women's Vigilance Committee, the Club of the Social Revolution, and the Club of the Revolution. There were also women's newspapers, such as the *Le Journal des Citoyennes de la Commune* (*Journal of the Citizens of the Commune*) and *La Sociale* (*Society*).

Activists

The Commune – unlike the revolutions of 1848 – saw many women come to prominence as feminists and as fighters. In particular, there were many more ordinary working women (especially seamstresses) as well as educated middle-class radicals. The best known include Louise Michel, who was the first to raise the warning on 18 March. Active in socialist politics and a member of the First International, she often presided over the Club of the Revolution. She was also an excellent rifle shot. After the Commune's defeat, she was transported to a penal colony. Another active socialist feminist was Elizabeth Dmitrieff, who had joined the International aged 17 and become a friend of Marx. She became one of the seven-strong executive committee of the Union of Women. She eventually escaped to Switzerland.

More of a Blanquist than a Marxist was André Léo, a feminist and excellent journalist who edited *La Sociale*. She, too, was forced into exile in Switzerland. Béatrix Excoffon was politically activated by the siege of Paris and in early April she helped organise a march by some 800 women which tried unsuccessfully to prevent Thiers' government from attacking the Commune. She was a member of the Women's Vigilance Committee, as were Sophie Poirier and Anna Jaclard. Excoffon and Poirier were later transported, while Jaclard escaped to Switzerland.

Mention should also be made of noted fighters such as Marie-Catherine Rigissart, a leader of the women's battalion; Adélaide Valentin and Louise Neckebecker, colonel and captain, respectively, of a company of women in the 12th Legion; and Blanche Lefebvre of the Union of Women, summarily executed for her part in the final battles.

Others who fought, were killed, or who were punished afterwards include: Jeanne Hachette, Victorine Louvet, Marguerite Lachaise, Nathalie Lemel, and, finally, Joséphine Courbois-Delettra, the Lyons heroine of 1848. Clearly, with so much more to gain than men from a successful revolution, these early feminists were determined to fight to the bitter end against the conservative status quo and their double oppression as workers and as women.

The Russian Revolution, 1917

Actions

The struggle for the emancipation of women was not a Bolshevik innovation – it had been an important part of the revolutionary tradition of the Russian radical intelligentsia since the 1860s. Many educated women had been active in Narodnik (or Populist) revolutionary circles in the 1870s and 1880s, and went on to participate fully in the revolutionary activities of the Social Revolutionaries. Such involvement included carrying out assassinations as well as agitating for specific feminist demands. (In 1878, for example, Vera Zasulich, a student, shot Colonel Trepov, the governor-general of St Petersburg.) Women were also at the forefront of the various Marxist groups which eventually became the Russian Social Democratic Labour Party, while many were active in the 1905 Revolution.

From 1910, there was a tremendous growth amongst working women of militancy, organisation and awareness of their specific needs. These developments, which had begun to shatter the traditional image of women as the most politically backward and conservative section of society, were intensified by the outbreak of war in 1914, which saw a huge increase in the number of women working in factories. The highpoint of this process can be seen in the role of women in precipitating the March Revolution of 1917.

Russia's disastrous performance in the First World War had resulted in the introduction of flour and bread rationing in Petrograd in 1916, and rumours of serious shortages had led to bread riots. In addition, the Putilov workers had been locked out by their employers on 7 March. The following day, International Women's Day, saw a huge women's demonstration mainly by women of the Vyborg district, which greatly added to the number of women on the streets. The demonstration went beyond demanding sufficient supplies of food, to raise political demands such as an end to the war, and the overthrow of the monarchy. The next day, women stayed on the streets and helped organise the protests and general strike which ended in revolution a few days later.

After the March Revolution, feminists struggled hard for two months to ensure that the provisional government gave the vote to all women, as well as to men. For the next few months, however, most women tended to play a more passive, and less specifically feminist, role. This was partly because many revolutionary groups – including, for a time, the Bolsheviks – saw separate women's sections as divisive, and a distraction from the broader political struggles. Nonetheless, many threw themselves into revolutionary activity, such as organising the printing and distribution of party leaflets and newspapers, planning demonstrations and, occasionally, addressing mass meetings and rallies. Even amongst the Bolsheviks, however, women played a relatively minor role in the November Revolution itself, though women supporters of Kerensky and his provisional government did organise the Women's Death Battalions to help defend the Winter Palace.

Organisations

The main non-Bolshevik women's groups were the League of Equal Rights and the League of Women's Equality, mainly middle-class feminist movements, which campaigned hard from March to May 1917 to ensure women were given the right to vote. They organised a 40,000-strong women's demonstration and, in April, held an All-Russian Congress of Women. This, in turn, set up the Republican Union of Democratic Women's Organisations to continue the campaign for women's suffrage. Many non-Bolshevik feminists supported the continuation of Russia's war effort after March 1917, and set up the National Council of Women. It was this group in particular which supported the creation of Women's Death Battalions.

The Bolsheviks were initially reluctant to establish a separate women's organisation, despite the strong suggestions of many women members. However, they did support the Rabotnitsa group, which was set up in 1914, organised working-class women, and produced the newspaper *Rabotnitsa* (*The Working Woman*). This group developed a network of ties with factories and other workplaces in the major cities, and was able to hold large meetings which popularised both Bolshevik slogans and feminist demands.

The success of the Rabotnitsa group finally persuaded the Bolsheviks, in 1919, to set up a special Communist Party women's department, Zhenotdel, with the aims of organising and educating women, protecting their interests and helping them play an independent role. Although funds were very short, they still managed to organise several congresses and make many proposals for the communual provision of private domestic functions, such as public canteens, laundries and child-care centres. Finally, in 1930, Stalin disbanded Zhenotdel, and the Proletarian Women's Movement came to an end. Instead, the more conservative and traditional aspects of the family and women's roles were emphasised.

Activists

The most significant non-communist feminists were Vera Figner, a leader of the revolutionary People's Will group in the 1880s who went on to lead the fight for women's suffrage after March 1917; Ekaterina Kaskova, active in the League for Women's Equality and the co-operative movement, and editor of the *Vlast' Narodna* (*Power of the People*) newspaper; and Maria L. Bochkareva, who was behind the establishment of the Women's Death Battalions, and commanded the unit defending the Winter Palace in November 1917.

Social Revolutionary activists included Ekaterina Breshko-Breshkovskaya and the legendary Maria Spiridonova, who was one of the main leaders of the Left

SRs and who, in 1918, ordered the assassination of the German ambassador, Mirbach, in an attempt to prevent the Treaty of Brest-Litovsk.

Angelica Balabanoff, who initially followed a political path similar to that of Alexandra Kollontai, a left-wing Menshevik Internationalist, eventually split from the Bolshevik regime and went into exile in 1924.

The most significant Bolshevik feminist was Alexandra Kollontai. A member of the Russian Social-Democratic Labour Party (RSDLP) from the age of 17, she was active in the 1905 Revolution, though she initially supported the Mensheviks in the 1903 split. In 1914 she joined the Bolsheviks, helped edit their women's newspaper, *The Working Woman*, and went on to become the only woman to be a full member of the Bolshevik central committee. She voted for insurrection and, after November 1917, became commissar for social welfare. As commissar, she was able to introduce laws to further women's emancipation and equality. Associated with the left-wing communists in the arguments over the Treaty of Brest-Litovsk, she resigned as commissar, and became the director of Zhenotdel in 1920. However, seeing the dangerous growth of bureaucracy before Lenin, she went on to become a prominent leader of the Workers Opposition faction, writing and printing their pamphlet for the 10th Party Congress in 1921. Yet she is probably best known for the misrepresentation of her views on the family and sexual relationships – many accused her of promoting promiscuity.

Other prominent communist women include Nadezhda Krupskaya and Zlata Lilina – both active in their own right before they married their better-known revolutionary husbands (Lenin and Zinoviev, respectively). Krupskaya, initially a supporter or member of People's Will, became a Marxist in 1891, helped organise strikes in 1895, and went on to act as secretary and accountant of the newspaper *Iskra* (*The Spark*) from 1903 and then of the Bolsheviks from 1903 until 1917. She also became the Bolsheviks' expert on producing false passports. Her place as secretary was taken by Elena Stasova, another revolutionary active since the 1890s, who became an alternate member of the Bolshevik central committee in 1917, along with Varvara Iakovleva, who also voted for insurrection in October 1917.

Many communist women were active in the Rabotnitsa group. As well as Kollontai and Krupskaya, there were Inessa Armand, who went on to be the first director of Zhenotdel, and Liudmilla Stalh, who, during the civil war, edited Red Army newspapers and worked in the political sections of the army. Both these women were active in Marxist politics at an early age. Tatiana Ludvinskaya, a Bolshevik since 1903, was wounded in barricade fighting in the 1905 Revolution, and went on to take part in the revolutionary take-over in Moscow in November 1917.

Older Marxist revolutionaries such as Vera Zasulich, the assassin of Trepov, who went on to help found the RSDLP, and Clara Zetkin, who greatly influenced Kollontai on the need to organise working-class women, should also be mentioned.

The various political and social struggles waged, the demands raised, and the examples given by such female Russian revolutionaries proved to be significant models for feminists throughout Europe and beyond. Many of the feminist movements which developed in the 1960s and 1970s consciously sought inspiration from the activists and ideas that emerged in Russia during the turmoil of the 1917 Revolution.

Revolutionary women in France, 1789–93

8.1 The Rights of Woman

Olympe de Gouges documented and presented this Declaration of the Rights of Women, October? 1791

Man, are you capable of being just? . . . Go back to animals, consult the elements, study plants, finally glance at all the modifications of organic matter, and surrender to the evidence when I offer you the means; search, probe, and distinguish, if you can, the sexes in the administration of nature. Everywhere you will find them mingled; everywhere they cooperate in harmonious togetherness in this immortal masterpiece . . .

Declaration of the Rights of Woman and the Female Citizen

For the National Assembly to decree in its last sessions, or in those of the next legislature:

Preamble

Mothers, daughters, sisters [and] representatives of the nation demand to be constituted into a national assembly.

Consequently, the sex that is as superior in beauty as it is in courage during the sufferings of maternity recognizes and declares in the presence and under the auspices of the Supreme Being, the following Rights of Woman and of Female Citizens.

Article I

Woman is born free and lives equal to man in her rights. Social distinctions can be based only on the common utility.

Article VI

The law must be the expression of the general will; all female and male citizens must contribute either personally or through their representatives to its formation; it must be the same for all: male and female citizens, being equal in the eyes of the law, must be equally admitted to all honors, positions, and public employment according to their capacity and without other distinctions besides those of their virtues and talents.

Article X

No one is to be disquieted for his very basis opinions; woman has the right to mount the scaffold; she must equally have the right to mount the rostrum, provided that her demonstrations do not disturb the legally established public order.

Article XIII

For the support of the public force and the expenses of administration, the contributions of woman and man are equal; she shares all the duties [*corvées*] and all the painful tasks; therefore, she must have the same share in the distribution of positions, employment, offices, honors, and jobs [*industrie*].

Source: D. G. Levy, H. B. Applewhite and M. D. Johnson (eds.), *Women in revolutionary Paris, 1789–1795*, Illinois, 1979, pp. 89–91

8.2 Women demand equal rights

Report of the proceedings of the Legislative Assembly

1 April 1792

'The former Baronne d'Aelders, a Dutch woman, accompanied by several other women, is admitted to the bar. After a long eulogy of feminine virtues, after having maintained that women equal men in courage and in talent, and almost always surpass them in imagination, she requests that the Assembly take into consideration the state of degradation to which women find themselves reduced as far as political rights are concerned, and reclaims on their behalf the full enjoyment of the natural rights of which they have been deprived by a protracted repression. To attain this objective, she asks that women be admitted to civilian and military positions and that the education of young people of the feminine sex be set up on the same foundation as that of men. Women have shared the dangers of the Revolution; why shouldn't they participate in its advantages?

The president answers the petitioners that the Assembly will avoid, in the laws it is entrusted with making, everything that might provoke their regrets and their tears, and grants them the honours of the session. (The Assembly sends the petition to the joint Committees on Legislation and Education.)'

Source: L. Kekewich and S. Rose, *The French Revolution*, London, 1990, pp. 59–60

(Note that granting them 'the honours of the session' was a mere formality which, in effect, meant the petitioners would be ignored.)

8.3 Women and the *taxation populaire* of February 1793

Not only were there threats to the government from the frontiers and provinces, there was also mounting discontent in Paris, for high prices and unemployment had driven hordes of the hungry to the capital in search of work. Inflation, a consequence of the vast numbers of *assignats* issued to finance the war, pushed up prices. Early in 1793 the cost of a wide range of consumer goods increased rapidly. Soap, for example, essential for the work of thousands of laundry women, had reached 23–28 *sous* compared with 12 *sous* in 1790. On 25 and 26 February grocers' and chandlers' shops were raided by market women who sold goods off at what they considered to be a fair price, although there was also a considerable amount of pillaging. A delegation of washerwomen demanded the death penalty for hoarders. This agitation owed little to the Montagnards, but was rather spontaneous action by women who found it difficult to feed their families. Robespierre rather sniffily criticised the *menu peuple* for being more concerned with 'vulgar groceries' than the power struggle in the Convention . . .

For a brief period the *enragés* came to prominence with a programme of controlled grain prices as a preliminary step towards a general *Maximum* . . .

Jacques Roux, the most prominent *enragé*, was one of the most attractive characters of the Revolution. A priest in one of the poorest Paris *sections*, with a following in the Cordeliers Club, he was genuinely appalled by the poverty and hardship suffered by the common people; hardship that was now so much greater than before 1789. Lacking all personal ambition and deficient in political skills, he wanted something done about the high cost of living *(la vie chère)*. In fact the *enragés* consisted only of three to five people, of whom Roux and Jean-François Varlet were the only two who really mattered. An extremist splinter group of *sans culotte* militants, they demanded economic justice, especially food for all, and condemned those who were making a comfortable living out of the Revolution. Roux, one of the few who was not in the Revolution for what he could get out of it, spoke for the very poorest of Parisians and could not be bought off or his dangerous doctrines silenced.

Source: D. G. Wright, *Revolution and terror in France, 1789–95*, 2nd edn, London, 1990, pp. 66–67

8.4 A meeting of the Society of Revolutionary Republican Women

Notes taken by Pierre Joseph Alexis Roussel during a visit to a meeting of the Society of Revolutionary Republican Women, autumn 1793, with Lord Bedford as his companion

When we came in, the session had just begun. Before describing it I will say that some of these women covered their heads with red caps, in particular the president and the secretaries. This grotesque spectacle almost choked us, because we felt constrained not to let ourselves burst out laughing. This session seemed so comical to us that we each made a separate record of it when we left, while our memories were still filled with these details. All I am doing is copying our notes.

Session of the Society of Women,
Meeting in the Ossuary of the Church of Saint-Eustache

Presidency of Citoyenne Lacombe

After the reading of the minutes and of the correspondence, the president recalled that the order of the day concerned the utility of women in a republican government, and she invited the sisters who had worked on this subject to share their research with the Society. Sister Monic was given the floor and read what follows:

> From the famous Deborah, who succeeded Moses and Joshua, to the two Frei sisters, who fought so valiantly in our republican armies, not a single century has passed which has not produced a woman warrior . . . Joan of Arc, who forced the English to flee before her, shamed them into raising the siege of Orleans, and the name of that city is added to hers.

Without my having to cite for you the individual names of the courageous female warriors . . . I call your attention to the *citoyennes* of Lille, who, at this moment, are braving the rage of assailants and, while laughing, are defusing the bombs being cast into the city. What do all these examples prove, if not that women can form battalions, command armies, battle, and conquer as well as men?

Source: D. G. Levy, H. B. Applewhite and M. D. Johnson (eds.), *Women in revolutionary Paris, 1789–1795*, Illinois, 1979, pp. 166–67

8.5 The Society of Revolutionary Republican Women and the *Enragés*

Report of a meeting of the Jacobin Club, stressing the connection between Claire Lacombe (president of the SRRW) and Leclerc, an Enragé

Session of Monday, September 16, 1793

Leonard Bourdon as President

(A *secretary* announces that the Society of Revolutionary Women took the side of Leclerc, friend of Jacques Roux; Citoyenne Lacombe, President of this Society, wrote to Citoyenne Goven, Leclerc's denouncer, to summon her to come to explain her conduct . . . Basire asserts, as Chabot already had, that these women spoke with scorn of 'Monsieur Robespierre, who dared to treat them as counterrevolutionaries.')

A *citizen* begins by attributing to women all the disorders which have occurred in Paris. The galleries complain, but he ends by asking for the arrest of *muscadines* as well as muscadins. The entire Society applauds.

Taschereau says that Citoyenne Lacombe meddles everywhere; at an assembly where the speaker was present, she asked first for the constitution, the whole constitution, only the constitution, and you will note in passing this hypocritical and Feuillant language; after that she wanted to sap the foundation of the constitution and overturn all kinds of constituted authorities.

These two propositions are put to the vote: (1) to write to the Revolutionary Women to engage them to rid themselves by a purifying vote of the suspect women who control the Society; (2) to send [word] to the Committee of General Security to commit it to having suspect women arrested. (Decided unanimously.) This amendment is made: that Citoyenne Lacombe be taken immediately before the Committee of General Security. (There is applause.) There is also [an amendment] to ask the Committee for Leclerc's arrest.

Chabot: You cannot indict just any citizen before the Committee of General Security, but you may ask the Committee of General Security to summon the Lacombe woman, because I do not have any doubt that she is the instrument of counterrevolution.

Source: D. G. Levy, H. B. Applewhite and M. D. Johnson (eds.), *Women in revolutionary Paris, 1789–1795*, Illinois, 1979, pp. 182–4

8.6 Opposition to the radicalism of the Society of Revolutionary Republican Women

An account of the meeting of the SSRW, 7 Brumaire (28 October) 1793

While they were waiting for the members to arrive, a *citoyenne* reported to those present in the room concerning the measures our enemies were taking to starve patriots. She reported on what had just been found in the sewers of Montmartre and the Temple – a large quantity of bread . . . Several people attested to the truth of the statement. Others cried out, 'Down with red bonnets! Down with Jacobin women! Down with Jacobin women and the cockades! They are all scoundrels who have brought misfortune upon France!' . . . Six citizens arrived, sabres unsheathed, along with the justice of the peace, named Lindet, who entered the gallery. He asked for the floor; the President gave her consent. He said, '*Citoyennes*, in the name of the law, silence; in the name of the law I order you to stop talking.' Then he said, '*Citoyennes*, what's at issue is not the red bonnet; you will stop wearing it, and you will be free to put whatever you wish on your heads.' Then the people in the galleries applauded with the greatest outburst of feeling. The justice of the peace, addressing himself to the spectators, said to them: 'The *citoyennes révolutionnaires* are not in session; everyone can come in.' At this point a crowd of countless numbers of people came into the room and heaped the filthiest abuse upon the members . . . The *citoyennes*, unfaltering in the midst of dangers, not wanting to abandon their symbols, were struck and most shamefully attacked.

Source: D. G. Levy, H. B. Applewhite and M. D. Johnson (eds.), *Women in revolutionary Paris, 1789–1795*, Illinois, 1979, pp. 209–11

8.7 The banning of the Society of Revolutionary Republican Women

An account of the report of the Committee of General Security, presented by André Amas, to the National Convention, on the disturbances of 7 Brumaire, and the decision of the Convention to ban the Society of Revolutionary Republican Women, 9 Brumaire (30 October) 1793

National Convention
Moise Bayle, Presiding
Session of 9 Brumaire

. . . *Amar, for the Committee of General Security*: Citizens, your Committee has been working without respite on means of warding off the consequences of disorders which broke out the day before yesterday in Paris at the Marché des Innocents, near Saint-Eustache . . . Several women, calling themselves Jacobins, from an allegedly revolutionary society, were going about in the morning, in the market and under the ossuaries of les Innocents, in pantaloons and red bonnets. They intended to force other *citoyennes* to wear the same costume; several [of the latter] testified that they had been insulted by them . . .

In the evening the same disturbance broke out with greater violence. A brawl started. Several self-proclaimed Revolutionary Women were roughed up. Some members of the crowd indulged themselves in acts of violence towards them which decency ought to have proscribed. Several remarks reported to your Committee show that this disturbance can be attributed only to a plot by enemies of the state. Several of these self-proclaimed Revolutionary Women may have been led astray by an excess of patriotism, but others, doubtless, were motivated only by malevolence.

Right now, when Brissot and his accomplices are being judged, they want to work up some disorders in Paris, as was the case whenever you [the Convention] were about to consider some important matter and when it was a question of taking measures useful for the Fatherland . . .

With respect to these two questions, the Committee decided in the negative . . .

We believe, therefore, and without any doubt you will think as we do, that it is not possible for women to exercise political rights. You will destroy these alleged popular societies of women which the aristocracy would want to set up to put them [women] at odds with men, to divide the latter by forcing them to take sides in these quarrels, and to stir up disorder . . .

The decree proposed by Amar is adopted in these terms:

The National Convention, after having heard the report of its Committee of General Security, decrees:

Article 1: Clubs and popular societies of women, whatever name they are known under, are prohibited. [Article] 2: All sessions of popular societies must be public.

Source: D. G. Levy, H. B. Applewhite and M. D. Johnson (eds.), *Women in revolutionary Paris, 1789–1795*, Illinois, 1979, pp. 213–17

Document case-study questions

1 What does Document 8.2 reveal about male attitudes to political activism by women?

2 From what you have read in this book and elsewhere, explain *briefly* the following references in Document 8.3: (a) *assignats*, (b) the Montagnards, (c) the *Enragés*.

3 How useful are Documents 8.1 and 8.4 as evidence of the political demands of women during the period 1789–95?

4 Assess the reliability of Documents 8.5, 8.6 and 8.7 as historical evidence of the activities of the Society of Revolutionary Republican Women (SRRW).

5 How far do these *seven* documents explain the reasons behind the decision of the Committee of General Security to ban the SRRW?

9 Reaction and counter-revolution

Introduction

Because all revolutions are determined attempts to radically alter existing social, economic and political systems, it is no wonder that there is always considerable opposition to such events. This opposition comes primarily from those with most to lose from any such transformations – political rulers, and those with substantial social and economic privileges. However, as was seen in Chapter 4, the ideas and values associated most strongly with dominant social groups have an influence which extends far beyond the ranks of such elites. It is this that enables such minority groups to find individuals and, sometimes, sizeable sections of society, to support their plans for conservative resistance, reaction and counter-revolution. In virtually every case, counter-revolution is an attempt to return to the pre-revolutionary status quo, although sometimes new ideas are also required to attract support for a counter-revolution.

There are various aspects associated with counter-revolutions, though all are not necessarily present in each case. Firstly, there is always violence. In almost every known case the violence of the counter-revolution has been far more bloody and extensive than that associated with the revolution. In part, this is because the traditional rulers and dominant groups are normally able to maintain control of existing or newly created professional military forces, with superior weapons. This military advantage is one of the main reasons why most revolutions are unsuccessful. The violence is also partly explained by a desire on the part of the dominant group to teach the insurgent masses a harsh lesson and so prevent future trouble.

Secondly, reaction and counter-revolution normally come in two phases in the revolutionary process: during the revolution itself, and, if the revolution is not defeated, following its collapse. In the course of a revolution, leaders and parties are often continuously on the look-out for the first signs of counter-revolution. At times, these fears lead to revolutionary terror in which even dissident revolutionaries are purged or suppressed, along with genuine reactionaries.

If a revolution is initially successful, there sometimes occurs a kind of creeping counter-revolution – this tends to happen when the new revolutionary regime is forced to cope with the practical realities of government. Very often, the disintegration of the old system leads to a style of crisis management which is often at variance with the original revolutionary ideals. If the support of the masses is weakened as a result, counter-revolution soon becomes a real possibility.

Finally, ever since the French Revolution of 1789, counter-revolution has tended to operate on two levels: domestically and internationally. As was seen in Chapter 7, from the eighteenth century onwards there has been a conscious attempt to spread revolutionary ideas and organisations across borders. It is hardly surprising that dominant and privileged elites in a particular country fight ruthlessly to protect their positions and possessions. However, they often also attempt to seek assistance from similar groups and regimes abroad. Usually, such support is readily forthcoming, as rulers in neighbouring states tend to be fully aware of what has been termed the 'threat of a good example'. This is especially true of periods which witnessed significant waves of revolution: 1789–95, 1848 and 1917–23.

Sometimes, despite all the immediate attempts at counter-revolution, and all the problems associated with constructing a new economic and social system, revolutionary regimes do survive. However, these tend to become isolated islands of revolution, surrounded by hostile and powerful states. Having failed to crush the revolution militarily, such states will attempt to secure the same result by a more lengthy process of economic pressure and strangulation. Thus even successful revolutionaries have found that the threat of counter-revolution never disappears, and requires constant revolutionary vigilance and struggle. This is something which is exceptionally difficult to maintain over a long period of time.

The French Revolution, 1789

Attempts at reaction and counter-revolution were present throughout the entire course of the French Revolution: three distinct phases can be identified, as described below.

1789–91

As early as June 1789, there were the first signs of a royalist counter-revolution when supporters of the court, led by Louis XVI's younger brother, the Comte d'Artois, and Charles de Barentin, tried to get the Third Estate's resolution setting up the National Assembly declared null and void. Though this attempt failed (about 30,000 Parisians had demonstrated in protest), the court continued to fight back: in July, Necker was dismissed as controller-general of finances and replaced by de Breteuil, a nominee of the queen; while loyal Swiss and German troops were ordered to Versailles. It was this that resulted in the formation of the National Guard and the storming of the Bastille.

Continued attempts at counter-revolution included Louis' initial refusal to accept the August decrees and the Declaration of the Rights of Man, and the various royalist and aristocratic plots to abduct the king and move him well away from Paris. When, in September, the Flanders Regiment was ordered to Versailles, and was greeted by a banquet organised by the royal Gardes-du-

Corps, the result was the October March to Versailles, which ended with Louis and the National Assembly being forced to move to Paris.

These early attempts at counter-revolution (which had actually helped push the revolution into more radical directions) were relatively bloodless. However, the 1791 Civil Constitution of the Clergy, which reduced the number of bishops and introduced the election of priests, gave rise to much more determined and violent resistance. For example, several areas saw some limited reactionary uprisings which were supported and encouraged by aristocratic *émigrés* and other supporters of Crown and Church.

1792–93

It was the outbreak of war with Austria in April 1792 which seemed to give counter-revolutionaries their best opportunity to date. The court – especially Marie-Antoinette and the Marquis de Lafayette (the first commander of the National Guard in 1789) – certainly hoped that the Girondins would lose the war, so enabling royalists to regain control. It was precisely such fears that led Robespierre to oppose the Girondin push for war. As was later shown when the crowds invaded the Tuileries in August 1792, the queen maintained communications with the Austrians, and with counter-revolutionaries in France, in what some revolutionaries saw as the beginnings of a European-wide attempt to strangle the revolution.

The Vendée and Chouan catholic-royalist risings, in West France and in Brittany respectively, were particularly serious. Here, counter-revolutionary violence was much more brutal and murderous, and counter-revolutionaries often co-operated with *émigrés* and foreign armies. The first revolt in Brittany in 1792, led by the Marquis de la Rouërie, was timed to coincide with the Prussian invasion. In addition to these revolts, there were many others in various parts of France, also in support of Church and monarchy. In fact, it was counter-revolutionary violence and atrocities and the danger of collaboration with foreign enemies which led to the formation of the Revolutionary Tribunal and the beginnings of the Jacobin Terror (see pp. 60–61). Before long, as many as 120,000 men in the Vendée were fighting against the revolutionary government. This revolt and that of the Chouans in Brittany were not finally defeated until 1796.

In addition to counter-revolution in the form of monarchists waging a bitter civil war, and an invasion spearheaded by Austria and by German princes, the period 1792–93 also saw more moderate revolutionaries beginning to have second thoughts. As early as July 1792, they attempted unsuccessfully to ban political clubs and societies, and many became increasingly concerned by the growing political independence of the sans-culottes and the lower classes. For a time, only Robespierre and his supporters were willing to maintain the momentum, and from then on, all who disagreed came to be seen as potential, if not actual, counter-revolutionaries.

1794–99

The length of the French Revolution presents a particular problem when it comes to assessing at what point it came to a close or, more precisely, when reaction and counter-revolution can be seen as having triumphed. Some historians argue that Robespierre's suppression of the Commune, the *Enragés* and then the Hébertists and Dantonists, in the period March–April 1794, marks the first step in counter-revolution. Many more see Thermidor, in July 1794, when Robespierre was overthrown (see p. 50), as the turning point for successful reaction and counter-revolution. Beginning with the execution of Robespierre and 21 of his supporters on 28 July, the Thermidorians went on to guillotine over 100 more Montagnards and Commune members in the space of a few days. The pace of executions then slowed down, to only 63 in the next ten months, though the Jacobin Club was closed and the popular protests and revolts of Germinal and Prairial 1795 were ruthlessly suppressed. Significantly, army leaders became increasingly important.

After Thermidor, there followed what has been called a White Terror, in which royalists and returned *émigrés*, along with alienated members of the wealthy middle classes, formed groups such as the Company of the Sun and the Company of Jesus to take revenge on Robespierrists and other members of the popular societies, political clubs and the *comités de survéillance*. In Lyons and the Rhône valley, there were prison massacres of Robespierre's supporters and other militants, similar to the September Massacres of 1792. Elsewhere, especially in *départements* of north-west and south-east France, there was considerable violence: in the south-east in 1795 groups of middle-class youths killed over 2,000 supporters of revolution; while over 1,000 republican prisoners were butchered by Chouan rebels in Brittany. Though this counter-revolutionary violence did not take place everywhere in France, it continued through 1796 and most of 1797. In Paris itself, the violence was more limited: middle-class gangs of the *jeunesse dorée* (gilded youth) and the *muscadins* (fops) mainly contented themselves with beating up Jacobins and anyone who looked like a possible sans-culotte militant, and there was relatively little serious bloodshed.

Despite these developments, the Thermidorian reaction was *not* a complete counter-revolution. On the contrary, they had themselves supported some of the Jacobins' measures, and generally wanted to return to the more moderate 1789–91 phase of the revolution. This was partly reflected by the new constitution of 1795, which set up the Directory, and a legislature of two Houses: the Council of the 500, and the Council of Elders. In elections in the spring of 1797, most seats were won by royalists and other conservatives, and laws were soon passed which were more sympathetic to *émigrés* and refractory priests (priests who refused to accept the Civil Constitution and its oath of loyalty to the nation). Soon, however, the Directory purged the monarchists, in the Fructidor Coup of 3–4 September.

If Thermidor was thus *not* a victorious counter-revolution, many would see the 18th Brumaire Coup of 9–10 November 1799, when Napoleon Bonaparte overthrew the Directory and set up the Consulate, as the final chapter of the

French Revolution, while others would argue that the end only finally came in 1804, when Napoleon declared himself emperor. Yet even then there was no attempt to revert to the pre-1789 situation, and most aspects of the revolution continued to survive, with the result that many see Napoleon's wars as both defending and extending the Revolution. Consequently, counter-revolution is seen as only finally triumphing following his defeat in 1814, which then allowed the restoration of the Bourbon monarchy in 1815.

The 1848 revolutions

Counter-revolutionary violence was much more limited in 1848 than in any of the other revolutions considered by this book. With the exception of events in France, there was none of the brutal repression associated with all subsequent counter-revolutions. In part, this can be explained by the fact that the revolutionary unity between the liberal middle classes and the more radical working classes very quickly collapsed. Within six months of the revolutions, counter-revolution was on the rise, and by the summer of 1849, was triumphant almost everywhere.

France

In the early stages of the 1848 revolution in France there was very little conservative resistance, as many in the middle classes were either very fearful or else considerably alienated from Louis Philippe's regime. Consequently, as members of the National Guard, they were reluctant to suppress the political disturbances which broke out in Paris and many of the other larger cities. In Paris itself, several regiments either handed over their weapons to the demonstrators or even joined them. This initial loss of military control meant it was virtually impossible to mount any effective repression, though, in fairness, it should be noted that the king refused to consider any such measures.

However, signs of an impending counter-revolution could be detected in the April elections for a new Constituent Assembly, which resulted in the majority of seats going to conservatives and royalists, or more moderate republicans. When the new government, which replaced the more radical provisional government, decided to end the National Workshops Scheme, a limited uprising in May was followed by the far more serious June Days. In the bitter street fighting that followed, government troops and the *gardes mobiles* (a special volunteer force linked to the National Guard) killed about 1,500 revolutionary insurgents. Further, the commander of the government's army, General Louis Eugène Cavaignac, then supervised a savage suppression in which a further 3,000 rebels were slaughtered and several thousand more were summarily transported – mostly to Algiers. Some contemporaries felt the barbarity of the government troops was even worse than that of the notorious Cossacks of Tsarist Russia. The author Victor Hugo commented that civilisation defended itself with the methods of barbarism. The new republican constitution which eventually emerged was clearly designed to alleviate the fears of property-owning moderates and conservatives. One thing was very obvious – military power was a crucial factor in this counter-revolution.

Habsburg Empire

As we saw in Chapter 3, the rapid development of revolutionary unrest took the Habsburg regime by surprise, and significant concessions were granted early on. However, following the emperor's flight in May, conservative supporters of the Habsburgs soon began to make preparations for a counter-revolution. Initially, the Italians and Czechs were to be the first victims, with Hungary and Austria to follow.

As the Italian states will be dealt with separately below, the Czech counter-revolution will be considered first. It was student and worker unrest in June 1848 in Prague which gave counter-revolution an early opportunity, when a riot on 12 June resulted in the accidental death of the wife of Prince Alfred Windischgrätz, the imperial governor of Moravia. Almost a week later, on 17 June, he began bombarding Prague into submission; he quickly took control of the city and became its military dictator. Significantly, the middle-class revolutionaries in Austria did not offer support to the Czech nationalists' revolution. The second crucial factor was that the authorities here (and elsewhere in the Habsburg Empire) had never lost control of their armies. In fact, no army anywhere during the revolutions of 1848 declared support for the various liberal constitutions drawn up by revolutionaries.

Early and easy success against the Czechs, which allowed the reconquest of the Bohemian lands (the economic centre of the empire), encouraged and enabled the Habsburg authorities to begin to take action against the revolutionaries in Hungary. The counter-revolution here was spearheaded by Count Joseph Jellačic, a chauvinistic Croat with a violent hatred of Magyars (Hungarians), who had been appointed governor of Croatia in March. In July, the Archduchess Sophie ordered Jellačic to suppress the Hungarian revolution, and his troops began their invasion in September.

This counter-revolutionary offensive also provided an opportunity for action against the revolutionaries in Vienna, when suspicion that troops from Vienna were to be sent to assist Jellačic in Hungary led to the October Days uprising. The events of this uprising frightened the wealthy into fleeing the city, and effectively ended the unity between middle-class and working-class revolutionaries. Windischgrätz, the conqueror of Prague, was given full powers to act: using the same method of bombardment as in Prague, he was able to regain control of Vienna – but only after some 5,000 people had been killed. However, although 1,600 insurgents were then arrested, only 9 were executed, while another 9 received long prison sentences.

Meanwhile, in Hungary, Jellačic's suppression of the revolutionaries – now led by Kossuth – met stubborn resistance and had to be reinforced by an army led by Windischgrätz. In January 1849, Windischgrätz's troops occupied Budapest and, in June, this counter-revolution was given international assistance by Tsar Nicholas I of Russia, who agreed to send in a large Russian army – undoubtedly because of the fear of similar developments in Russia's multi-ethnic empire. After the surrender of the Hungarians on 13 August 1849, Felix Schwarzenberg (Windischgrätz's brother-in-law and prime minister of Austria since November 1848) supervised a bloody repression – including the execution of Count Louis Batthyány and 13 army commanders. Worse was to follow when Baron Julius Jacob von Haynau replaced Windischgrätz as the new military commander. Haynau, who already had a brutal reputation and the nickname of 'Butcher', now carried out a murderous policy, which saw another 114 executions and over 2,000 prison sentences, and which caused the final collapse of the revolutionary movement in central and eastern Europe. Once again, military power had proved decisive.

German states

As in the Habsburg Empire, counter-revolution was given a chance after early revolutionary unity was undermined when increasingly independent and radical working-class movements began to frighten middle-class reformers. Many historians see the Schleswig-Holstein Question, April–August 1848, as an important turning point. In particular, Frederick William IV of Prussia – with the loyal support of his troops – began to mount a concerted effort to withdraw earlier concessions, and to reassert his authority. By November 1848, he had largely regained his previous powers. He was aided in this by the various workers' uprisings in Berlin, Elberfeld, and other Rhineland towns in the period March 1848 to May 1849, which in Germany, as elsewhere, quickly pushed middle-class reformers into the arms of conservatives and counter-revolutionaries. The counter-revolution in Germany, however, was less violent than that in the Habsburg Empire.

Italian states

Here, as in Hungary, revolutionaries were to hold out against counter-revolution longer than anywhere else. Earlier Austrian successes against Prague and Vienna enabled 30,000 troops to be sent to reinforce Marshal Radetzky's army in Italy, in June and July 1848. Almost immediately, a campaign was launched against Piedmont – the Austrian victory at Custozza clearly showing the importance of a reliable and well-equipped army. After this, division between middle-class moderates and radical peasants allowed Radetzky to carry out a successful counter-revolution in Lombardy, although radical republicanism and democracy continued to spread in many areas for some time after July 1848.

In February 1849 a republic was declared in Rome, which had been the main revolutionary centre in Italy since September 1848. Mazzini and Giuseppe Garibaldi now became particularly prominent. Here, however, the counter-revolution was carried out not by Austrian but by French troops, commanded by General Nicolas Oudinot. The Roman Republic finally ended in late June 1849 – once again as the result of military force.

By then, only Venice – which had been besieged and shelled since July 1848 – remained, along with Hungary, as a centre of revolutionary resistance in Europe.

Once again, it was the breakdown of revolutionary unity which finally allowed Radetzky's troops to force the city-republic to surrender, on 28 August 1849. Venice thus earned itself the claim to be the last survivor of the revolutions of 1848. By the autumn of 1849, Austrian control was fully re-established, and the counter-revolution was almost completely victorious.

In the end, across the whole of Europe it was essentially military power which finished off the revolutionary hopes of 1848 for liberal constitutions and national unity.

The Paris Commune, 1871

From the very beginning of the revolutionary Commune, in March 1871, its opponents in France had seen it as a 'new invasion of barbarians' and had feared some of the revolutionary ideas associated with it. They were especially alarmed by the threat to property rights posed by the 'spectre of communism' first mentioned by Marx in 1848. They were thus determined to crush it quickly, and in a way which would so decisively defeat such ideas that they would be removed from the political agenda for a very long time. It is clear that, rightly or wrongly, governments and ruling elites across Europe saw the *communards* as part of a growing and increasingly dangerous international labour movement which threatened their rule and their interests. This helps explain why the Prussians were so willing to assist in the suppression of the Commune.

Compared with the counter-revolutions of 1789–99 and 1848–49, this one was exceptionally bloody – even though total government casualties were little over 900. After the bitter street fighting came a systematic and premeditated process of summary executions and atrocities. Of the 25,000 or more *communards* who lost their lives in the fighting and in the subsequent slaughter, the vast majority were killed *after* resistance had ended. Though no official records were kept, the authorities in Paris itself paid for the burial or disposal of 17,000 corpses. These victims were mostly disposed of in mass graves or by mass burnings on pyres near the river. Many others were rounded up and marched off to prisons; many were shot for walking too slowly, while some officers simply selected prisoners at random for execution.

The generals who supervised this brutal savagery against male and female *communards* had a particular fear of radical republicanism, socialism and communism, and mistakenly tended to see Marx's First International as the main organiser of the Commune. Significantly, the government's troops fought far more viciously against these French men and women than they had against the Prussians. General Gaston Auguste Galliffet was notorious for selecting his victims according to whether they had watches or grey hair, or simply because he didn't like their faces. The Versailles captain who finally captured Montmartre had 42 men, 3 women and 4 children randomly selected for shooting.

Executions took place day and night: at La Roquette prison, 1,900 were shot in 2 days, while 400 were shot in the Mazas prison – none of these had had trials.

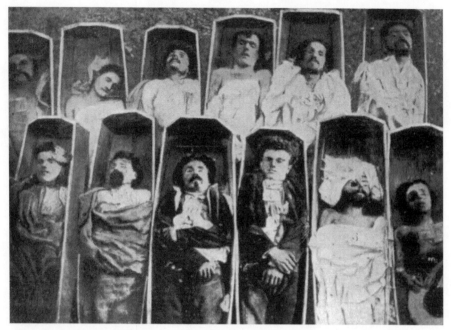

A photograph showing the corpses of some of the *communards* killed by Versailles troops after the defeat of the Commune in 1871. What does this photograph suggest about events in Paris following the government's victory?

The official trials, which lasted from August 1871 to January 1873, passed 270 sentences of death in all – 8 of those sentenced were women. In all, the Versailles government killed more French citizens than had died during the siege of Paris, or in the two years of Terror 1793–94. In addition, over 10,000 more were imprisoned, transported to penal colonies, or exiled. Most historians would accept that Thiers and his government were ultimately responsible for these outrages.

This 'revenge of the respectable people' horrified many people across the continent: on 29 May *The Times* commented on 'the inhuman laws of revenge under which the Versailles troops have been shooting, bayonetting, ripping up prisoners, women and children during the last six days . . . So far as we can recollect, there has been nothing like it in history.' As a comparison with the counter-revolutions of 1848–49 makes clear, these massacres were on a scale previously considered inconceivable in the more civilised states of nineteenth-century Europe. After 1871, the message was starkly clear to all revolutionaries involved in social revolutions which failed to maintain power.

The Russian Revolution, 1917

The Russian Revolution, even more than the French Revolution of 1789, presents a particular problem when we attempt to assess when counter-revolution took place, simply because of its considerable duration. Historians have identified a variety of different turning points: 1921, 1929, 1936–38 or even 1985–91.

One thing, however, is clear: from the very beginning, the Bolsheviks themselves expected to be quickly overthrown by counter-revolutionary forces, and initially merely hoped to survive long enough to help spark off the European revolution they believed would break out in the very near future. This view was not overly pessimistic and, in fact, attempts at counter-revolution – both internal and external – were to plague the new workers' state for decades to come. Two phases can be identified, as outlined below.

1917–21

In this early phase of the revolution, the disintegration of army discipline, and thus the speed of the collapse of the Tsarist regime in March 1917, for a time postponed attempts to plan a counter-revolution. However, the first serious signs of such plans can be seen in the events of the July Days, when reactionary and conservative forces apparently provoked the violence when they knew troops commanded by anti-soviet officers were approaching the capital. By then, plans for counter-revolution were being seriously discussed by senior military officers and leading industrialists, with the Kadets giving their support secretly. In the aftermath, Kerensky took the opportunity to ban the Bolsheviks, the largest and most revolutionary party in the soviets. Many saw this as simply the first step.

A much more serious and determined attempt at counter-revolution came in August 1917, with Kornilov's attempted coup. Kornilov, a die-hard conservative, had only recently been appointed as the new commander-in-chief by Kerensky, and there is some evidence to suggest that, at first, Kornilov was acting in conjunction with Kerensky. However, it soon became clear that Kornilov intended not only to sweep away the soviets and the revolutionary parties but also to overthrow the provisional government itself. Kerensky panicked when Kornilov refused to stop his advance, and appealed to the recently imprisoned Bolsheviks to assist. In the end, Kornilov was defeated without a shot being fired: the defensive actions taken by railway workers and by the revolutionary Red Guards in Petrograd, along with Bolshevik propaganda amongst Kornilov's troops, resulted in mass desertions the nearer they came to the capital. Though this attempt failed, it was fear of a more successful one which led Lenin, once the Bolsheviks had majorities in the major soviets, to push for a speedy second revolution.

Another aspect of attempted counter-revolution was the concerted pro-gramme of factory closures by owners who either locked out their workers or simply fled from the cities. This industrial sabotage greatly increased after November 1917.

It was after this November Revolution that preparations for counter-revolution became much more serious, especially after the signing of the Treaty of Brest-Litovsk in March 1918. There had already been armed resistance, and the newly elected Constituent Assembly had attempted to act as a focus for the growing counter-revolution. By the summer of 1918, a full-scale civil war had broken out.

As well as ending the coalition with the Left Social Revolutionaries, the signing of the treaty led to the formation of White Armies in Russia, which soon began to receive the support of expeditionary forces sent by several important capitalist countries. Though ostensibly sent merely to prevent Allied weapons from falling into German hands, these armies were soon involved on the side of the Whites. By 1918, the young Soviet state was clearly an unpleasant indication that the European status quo was not necessarily permanent.

These internal and external attempts at counter-revolution seemed destined for success, as the Bolsheviks controlled only the central core of Russia, and were surrounded by an apparently overwhelming array of White Armies, superior in both numbers and equipment. These were led by reactionary ex-Tsarist officers such as Admiral Alexander Kolchak, Generals Anton Denikin, Nikolai Yudenich and Peter Krasnov and, later, Baron Peter Wrangel. In addition, the 40,000-strong Czech Legion seized large parts of the Trans-Siberian Railway, while troops from Britain, France, Poland, Finland, Japan and the USA began to intervene in the civil war during the years 1918–20. A White Terror was launched against Bolsheviks and other revolutionaries, and against peasants who had seized landlords' estates. While records are patchy, it would appear that White atrocities were both more brutal and more extensive than the counter Red Terror undertaken by the Cheka, which had been formed in December 1917 to combat any counter-revolution.

However, this international attempt to strangle the new communist state at birth and restore reactionary Tsardom failed. This was partly because of Trotsky's skill in quickly establishing a massive and effective Red Army. But it was also partly because the peasantry knew that a victorious counter-revolution would mean that they would have to return land they had only recently taken or been given. Although the Bolsheviks survived this prolonged and bloody attempt at counter-revolution – much to everyone's surprise, theirs included – they were immediately faced with serious economic and political problems.

Attempts to deal with these problems led some left-wing communists, and non-Bolshevik revolutionaries, to accuse Lenin's government of instituting an internal creeping counter-revolution. Groups such as the Workers' Opposition and the Democratic Centralists saw growing bureaucratisation as undermining revolutionary socialist democracy, and such fears were greatly increased after the suppression of the Kronstadt Rising in 1921. Even more worrying to many was the New Economic Policy (NEP), which abandoned War Communism, and allowed market economics to reappear in agriculture and retail. The left-wing opponents of the NEP in fact began to call it the New Exploitation of the Proletariat. Just as worrying was the temporary ban on factions and other parties which followed almost immediately.

1922–38

To a large extent, these retreats from earlier revolutionary ideals had much to do with the tremendous legacy of destruction left by the counter-revolutionary civil war (e.g. the deaths of so many revolutionary workers who had been the first to volunteer for the Red Army). In addition, the isolation of the Bolshevik regime, both internally and externally, was increased after 1923. By then, it had become clear that the revolutionary wave which had spread across Europe after 1917 had passed. Despite early successes in several areas, by 1923 counter-revolution had defeated all revolutionary centres outside of Russia. In fact, Russia was now ringed by several countries ruled by hostile right-wing military dictatorships, while fascism – the most violent of all the reactionary and counter-revolutionary forces opposed to communism – had, in alliance with big business and property owners, already triumphed in Italy, and was beginning to spread elsewhere in Europe.

On top of these political and military threats, the new communist government was faced with an economic blockade, deliberately designed to further weaken the Soviet economy. If such economic warfare did not provoke an internal counter-revolution, then at least Russia would be less able to resist any future military intervention.

It was in this climate that Lenin's illness and subsequent death led to a power struggle in the period 1923–29. This contest was between leaders and sections of the Communist Party which, as in the past, divided into left, right and centre factions, with very different ideas and policies. By 1924, Trotsky was the leader of a Left Opposition, while Bukharin had moved to the right. For a time, the centre was led by Zinoviev, Kamenev and Stalin. Eventually – even though Zinoviev, Kamenev and, later, Bukharin, turned to Trotsky – Stalin was the one who triumphed. By 1929, all his leading opponents had been either removed from their government and party posts, expelled from the party or, in Trotsky's case, exiled from Russia itself.

Many saw – and still see – these developments, and the emergence of what became known as Stalinism, as indicating a triumphant conservative reaction, similar to that of Thermidor in the French Revolution of 1789 (see p. 102). While others have even described it as a capitalist restoration and thus a counter-revolution, especially after the show trials of 1936–38, which resulted in the execution, murder or suicide of virtually all the Bolshevik 'Old Guard' except Stalin. However, Trotsky himself never saw Stalin's triumph as a social and economic counter-revolution – though he certainly saw it as a conservative betrayal – despite the abandonment of several key revolutionary ideals. Instead, Trotsky saw it as a political take-over by an elite of administrators and officials. A new workers' *political* revolution would be needed in order to return to the communist road.

Whatever view is taken on the developments in Russia after 1924, it is clear that real and significant (though often contradictory) changes soon began to take place after Lenin's death. In particular, the destruction of democratic centralism in state and party, and the abandonment of international revolution, clearly signalled a falling away from the ideals and practices of the early phase of the Russian Revolution. However, unlike the counter-revolutions which ended the revolutions of 1789, 1848 and 1871, there was no restoration of the previous rulers.

Revolutionary continuity: victory and defeat

Introduction

Although a counter-revolution almost always results in the overthrow, and often the execution, of revolutionary leaders, some aspects of the revolution may well remain in place. Thus it is rare that the continuity of a revolution is completely broken by counter-revolution. This tends to hold true whether it is a counter-revolution from within the revolutionary movement itself, or a restoration of rulers and elites initially toppled by the revolution.

In the former case, despite often dramatic breaks with the original aims and practices of the revolution, counter-revolutionary leaders frequently claim to be acting in accordance with early revolutionary ideals. More importantly, at least some of the achievements and even the institutions of the revolution will survive – even if outward appearances are essentially a shell with little revolutionary content.

Even in the latter case, involving the return of pre-revolutionary elites, it is frequently impossible for such counter-revolutionary leaders to put the clock back completely: some of the revolutionary changes are able to survive counter-revolution and restoration, especially if the revolution has been a deep and prolonged event.

Thus, although revolutions often fall victim to a victorious counter-revolution – especially if their aims and aspirations are never fully achieved – it is not always a case of total defeat. Indeed, some of the incremental gains which survive the counter-revolution can provide a more favourable space for the growth of revolutionary possibilities than had existed before. This, and the political and organisational experiences gained during the revolutionary process, can result in a victorious and more long-lasting revolution the next time around. It is precisely here that revolutionary parties can play a key role by maintaining a collective memory of earlier revolutions in order to ensure continuity between revolutionary upheavals and the intervening periods of passivity and reaction.

The French Revolution, 1789

On one level, it is easy to claim that the 1789 revolution was clearly defeated, given that, after less than 20 years, the Bourbon monarchy and the great landowners returned in triumph in 1815, following Napoleon I's defeat and capture. Even before then, revolutionary continuity had been broken: first by Thermidor in 1794 then, in succession, by the emergence of the Consulate and the Empire. Any remaining influences of the revolution were further weakened in the fifty years after 1815, as France overthrew the Bourbons again in 1830; installed Louis Philippe and then later overthrew him in 1848; and then saw Louis Napoleon's coup of 1851, to be followed by his becoming Napoleon III during the Second Empire. Certainly, long before then, no rulers were claiming to be the political descendants of Robespierre and the Jacobins.

Furthermore, it is dramatically obvious that, after 1815, the Congress Powers as a whole tried simultaneously to restore the old order and to suppress the political and ideological currents which had raced across Europe after 1789. However, this victory of 1815 was more apparent than real, more one of outward appearance than inner substance. This was because, in the space of those twenty years of revolution and war, the old society had been disrupted and, at least partially, transformed beyond a point of no return. Above all, the ideals of 1789, and of 1792–94, became a permanent part of political debate throughout Europe.

In France itself, despite the restoration of the Bourbons and the subsequent conservative reaction, the revolution had successfully destroyed several features of the *ancien régime* for good. The Bourbons soon realised that some of the core accomplishments of the revolution, and especially of the Constituent Assembly, were permanent and irreversible.

Victory

Such irreversible victories fall into three main areas: politics/ideology, society and the economy.

Politics/ideology
The particular gain here was that it proved impossible to return fully to the idea of the divine right of kings and an absolute monarchy. It soon became clear, even to the Bourbons, that there was no way back to their past powers and glories. From now on, French people expected there to be an elected assembly with the right to pass laws. Furthermore, it was soon clear that the wealthier sections of the middle-class – the old Third Estate – were to play an increasingly significant role in politics. The new administrative system of *départements*, districts and *communes* also survived.

Society
Although the republic had been replaced by a returned monarchy, the pre-1789 aristocratic and hierarchical society (along with most of its institutions) had been shattered beyond repair. Returning *émigré* landowners, though able to regain ownership of about 25 per cent of the land they had lost, found the country had changed too much for them to restore any more than a shadow of their former power, privileges and prestige.

In particular, the middle classes and the wealthier peasants successfully retained the lands they had bought during the Revolution – whether these had been taken from the Church, or from *émigrés* and those suspected of supporting counter-revolution. These people now owned some 40 per cent or more of the land in France, which greatly increased their social status and influence. They were also able to ensure that the principle of the career 'open to talent', and the more rational and liberal legal, religious and educational systems constructed after 1789, survived the counter-revolution.

Economy

The revolutionaries of 1789–94, though no longer in power, were also victorious in the long run, in the sense that they had succeeded in wiping out the remnants of feudalism. Although it is possible to argue that the French economy before 1789 was already moving in the direction of a capitalist economy, the fact that it continued to do so after 1789 – and at a much faster rate – owed a great deal to the actions of 1789–91. The economic barriers resulting from feudal privilege and local customs duties, and the old taxes, were swept away for good, thus enabling a single national market to develop. Especially important here were the abolition of the old internal customs barriers, the feudal dues, and the restrictive practices of the guild system. This was also helped by the revolutionary reform of decimalisation, which established a uniform system of weights and measures.

Defeat

However, for the sans-culottes, and for urban workers and the poor – all of whom had played leading roles in 1789, 1792 and 1793–94 – revolutionary gains had begun to disappear after Thermidor. The rise of Napoleon and then the return of the Bourbons merely consolidated their defeat. For example, the price controls they had long demanded and finally achieved (via the Law of the General Maximum) had quickly been replaced after 1794 by a return to the 'free' market economy desired by the wealthy middle classes. In addition, they also lost the right to vote, which they had only briefly enjoyed. Their attempts at uprising in Germinal and Prairial 1795 were crushed; their discontent, however, continued after 1815 and rose to the surface again in 1848 and 1871.

Another revolutionary defeat came in 1796, when Babeuf's egalitarian conspiracy was also crushed. In the long term, however, this defeat did not mean the total elimination of revolution. On the contrary, Babeuf had begun to develop primitive socialist theories, and to link these with the Jacobin traditions of direct democracy, popular action, and insurrection. Quite clearly for his supporters, and for later socialists, Thermidor and its aftermath and then the Bourbon restoration meant the 1789 revolutionary slogans of liberty, equality and fraternity still remained to be achieved – even if the middle classes now thought otherwise. For those people who remained committed to the gains of 1792–94, only another revolution would bring them the popular democracy and the economic equality they continued to desire. Though temporarily defeated, many began almost immediately to resume the revolutionary struggle.

The 1848 revolutions

Unlike the French Revolution of 1789, which lasted some 5, 10 or 25 years – depending on whether 1794, 1799 or 1814 is taken as the closing date – most of the Revolutions of 1848 lasted barely a year. For this reason, the evidence for victory is slim, while that for defeat is overwhelming. Yet, even these were not total defeats, and the revolutions of 1848 managed to achieve some irreversible victories, such as the abolition of the remnants of the feudal system in many states and a significant long-term push towards the establishment of more liberal, parliamentary and democratic governments.

As we have seen in Chapter 9, a major reason for these sudden collapses and defeats was the rapid breakdown in the united opposition fronts established early on in 1848. Another important factor was that, in most states (with the exceptions of Hungary and the Roman Republic) the majority of peasants either remained indifferent to, or became hostile towards, the liberal, democratic and revolutionary aims of 1848. This cycle of victory and defeat will now be examined in the four key geographic areas of Europe during those sixteen months of revolution.

France

The most obvious victory of the February 1848 Revolution was in the political/ideological sphere: universal male suffrage, one of the main liberal republican aims to emerge in the 1789 Revolution, was achieved, on 2 March. This reform, which gave the vote to some 9 million new voters, was passed by the new provisional government led by Alphonse Lamartine, and had been a major demand in the February Revolution. Significantly, this revolutionary gain, though initially undermined in 1850, was reinstated after Louis Napoleon's coup in December 1851, and survived his declaration of the Second Empire a year later.

However, many of the leaders of February 1848 had wanted liberal reforms rather than a republican insurrection; they thus tended to assume that universal suffrage and the creation of a republic would satisfy everyone. Consequently, there was no attempt to alter the social and economic status quo, apart from the short-lived National Workshops Scheme to help alleviate the problems of unemployment. It was this failure to satisfy the social and economic demands of the workers, who had brought about the February Revolution, which led to the June Days uprising. Ironically, though Louis Napoleon destroyed the republic in 1852, his more authoritarian Decennial Republic and his Second Empire achieved more in the areas of social and economic reform.

The most obvious aspect of defeat was that the republic survived less than five years, before Louis Napoleon ended it in 1852. Yet within 20 years it was restored – this time for good. Also defeated were the ideals and movements desiring a social and more democratic republic, following the savage repression after the uprising of the June Days. However, despite defeat, the radical political groups had come to realise that it was unwise to put all their trust in liberal leaders. After 1848, a strong impetus was given to the creation of independent working-class socialist movements.

Habsburg Empire

Here, the liberal constitutions and nationalist aspirations of 1848 were very short-lived, and the picture after 1849 is one of almost total defeat. The only significant victories were in the social and economic spheres: the emancipation of the peasants from the Robot (feudal labour service) survived the counter-revolutions of 1849; while the Empire became a single economic market after the abolition of all internal customs barriers.

Politically, however, absolute and authoritarian monarchy seemed more powerful than ever after 1849, especially after the reactionary Franz-Joseph came to the throne. Although the new constitution drafted by Count Francis Stadion, which replaced the liberal Kromeriz Constitution, did include the liberal demand of equality before the law, most liberal political hopes were dashed during the neo-conservative era which followed the revolution. Even though subsequent Habsburg rulers did implement several liberal demands for the modernisation of their administrative system, the Habsburg Empire survived as a conservative and illiberal state until the First World War.

Also clearly defeated after 1849 were the nationalist hopes which had especially flourished amongst the Czechs and the Hungarians. Yet, even here, there was not total defeat: in particular, the continued strength of Hungarian nationalist sentiments resulted, in less than 20 years, in the autonomy provided by the Dual Monarchy of 1867. Other national groups, however, had to wait for the Habsburg defeat in 1918.

The more radical hopes and demands of the lower classes were ignored, as they were in France and elsewhere in Europe after 1849.

German states

As with the Habsburg Empire, the period after 1849 saw little victory, and almost total defeat, for the revolutionary hopes of 1848. The main revolutionary victory was economic, as the revolutions of 1848 did succeed in sweeping away the remnants of feudalism. This was confirmed by the king of Prussia, for instance, in 1850.

Politically, however, liberalism and liberal nationalism were comprehensively defeated by conservative counter-revolution – especially as many liberals, frightened by the revolutionary stirrings of the workers, saw traditional authority as their only saviour. In Prussia, for example, Frederick William IV dismissed his liberal ministers as early as October 1848, and dissolved the Berlin Assembly two months later. The appointment of Otto von Manteuffel as minister of the interior signalled the impending defeat of liberalism and the revival of monarchical autocracy. This resurgence of monarchical power was destined to flourish in the Prussia of William I and Bismarck. Socially, society remained extremely hierarchical, conservative and unequal.

In Prussia, and elsewhere in Germany, the middle classes were too small and too conservative for liberalism to survive the counter-revolution. In Prussia, for instance, although a constitution of sorts was granted in 1849 following the restoration of the old regime, it was replaced almost immediately, in 1850, by a much more monarchical and conservative one that lasted until the end of the First World War. For similar reasons, the Frankfurt Assembly, created by liberal nationalists, also collapsed. German nationalism in the future was to be a much more conservative, and even racist, phenomenon. Yet, within 25 years, their nationalist dream of a united Germany was achieved, though on the basis of 'blood and iron', not liberal idealism.

Italian states

As elsewhere, the story after 1849 is essentially one of revolutionary defeat rather than victory, as liberal constitutions were overthrown and Austrian political rule re-established. There were thus no obvious victories for Italian liberals and nationalists. Yet, even here, the defeats were not permanent: Austria's defeat by Prussia in 1866 meant that, in less than 20 years after 1848, national unification was finally achieved in Italy. Although, as with German nationalism, this was on a much more conservative basis than the liberal nationalism of 1848.

Another partial victory was the continuation of a more constitutional monarchy in Piedmont, especially under Charles Albert's successor, Victor Emmanuel II. However, elsewhere in Italy, rulers were able to revert to pre-revolutionary autocracy as, for example, in the kingdom of the Two Sicilies. Nevertheless, in Italy too, most of these rulers realised it was necessary to follow some of the liberal suggestions for modernising their administrative systems.

Summary

Despite the apparently overwhelming defeat of the revolutionary aspirations of 1848, revolutionary continuity was not completely broken and some revolutionary gains did survive after 1849. Even though the regimes which regained control after the defeat of the revolutions were essentially conservative or even reactionary, there was no return to the Europe of Metternich and the Congress System.

Politics, after 1848, became even more central, with the emergence of better-organised parties, programmes and ideologies. As a consequence, Europe became more political than ever before, and the opportunity for political debate was considerably extended. In future, though autocratic rulers might continue to oppose liberal, nationalist and democratic demands, these were now permanent features of the political landscape and could no longer be safely ignored by them. Even the Prussia of Bismarck had to make some concessions to parliamentary democracy.

Furthermore, one revolutionary thread which emerged from the defeats of 1849 was the development of a more scientific and revolutionary socialism, especially that based on the ideas of Karl Marx. Feeling ignored and then betrayed by middle-class liberals, future revolutionary democrats and socialists determined to fight for their ideals and interests independently of such lukewarm and unreliable allies, who clearly feared anything that looked like social revolution. Though these revolutionary-left working-class movements were not strong enough in 1848 to achieve their aims, they continued to develop after

1849, and became much more serious forces in the decades that followed.

In the short-term, however, the defeat of such revolutionary movements seemed total: in the years before 1914, violent social upheavals virtually disappeared from Europe. It was to take the turmoil caused by war to give social revolution another chance – in the Paris Commune of 1871, and the Russian Revolutions of 1905 and 1917. The continuity of such proletarian revolutionary ideals – stretching back to 1792–94 – was far from being broken by the defeats of 1849.

The Paris Commune, 1871

Of the four revolutions in the period 1789–1917, the Paris Commune is unique in that, following its bloody suppression, there is virtually no evidence of even a trace of victory. On the contrary, its defeat seemed total and, as Thiers had intended, the confidence of working-class leaders and movements seemed crushed beyond repair. In fact, the extent of the defeat did, for some time to come, slow down the development of revolutionary parties. To some, the Commune now seemed to be the last, albeit spectacular, attempt to keep alive a revolutionary tradition stretching back to the Jacobins and the sans-culottes. This revolutionary continuity was pronounced archaic and, now, defeated and dead for ever.

However, many continued to be alarmed at the prospect that democracy might eventually allow the working-class majority to remove bourgeois wealth and power. Yet, despite this obvious fear and the hatred felt by Thiers and the possessing classes for 'the vile multitude', the 1848 revolutionary gain of universal male suffrage remained intact. Furthermore, though there was no immediate hope of another Commune, surviving *communards* began to work, almost immediately, through various socialist parties in order to continue the struggle for their ideals.

More importantly, and more long-term, the Commune – despite its quick defeat – achieved a form of victory in that it has been an inspiration for revolutionaries across Europe, and even on other continents, ever since. Its manifesto had proclaimed 'the end of the old world', and many throughout the world were encouraged by the fact that, in the aftermath of war and in the midst of civil war, a government of working men and women could co-operate and govern themselves. Though it lasted only 72 days, its actions and ideals were closely studied, and its lessons assimilated and spread, by Marx and Engels and, later, by Lenin and the Bolsheviks. As late as 1936–39, revolutionaries in Spain claimed to be maintaining continuity with *communard* traditions and practices.

As a consequence, though physically defeated, the Commune and its political practice gave an added impetus to the continuity of social revolution. Revolution-ary horizons and possibilities were permanently widened as, for the first time, the elements of revolutionary ideals, a workers' government in power, and a conscious attempt to be relevant to people the world over, were combined in one spectacular revolutionary upheaval. Neither for the first nor the last time, revolutionary defeat would prove to be a valuable lesson, enabling future revolutionary victories – most notably, the Russian Revolution of 1917. Though the battle for the Commune was lost in 1871, the revolutionary struggle for its radical ideals was far from over.

The Russian Revolution, 1917

Of the four revolutions in the years 1789–1917 and, indeed, of all modern revolutions, the Russian Revolution of November 1917 is unique in at least two major respects. Firstly, it is possible to argue that it survived, in one form or another, for almost 75 years. Secondly, it is unprecedented in that it maintained at least a semblance of revolutionary continuity with regard to economic and social transformations, political institutions and commitment to its ideological traditions.

Although, as we saw in Chapter 9, this continuity seemed at least weakened, if not broken, at several points before the final collapse of the Soviet Union in 1991, one striking feature of the Russian Revolution is that even Gorbachev in the late 1980s claimed to be acting in accordance with the revolutionary ideals of 1917. Defeat can thus be seen as only occurring in 1991.

Victory

The prolonged victory of the November Revolution of 1917 can be detected in three broad areas, as outlined below.

Politics and ideology

One major political result of the Bolshevik revolution was the consolidation and formalisation of a system of government based on soviet democracy. This process of direct democracy (which overthrew the indirect representative democracy of the March Revolution and its belated Constituent Assembly) was based on a system of local soviets, at various political levels, culminating in an All-Russian Congress of Soviets, to which the Soviet government – at least in theory – was ultimately answerable.

This system almost immediately became one of the Russian Revolution's most significant contributions to revolutions and revolutionaries throughout the world. Though the actual practice soon became increasingly bureaucratic, the outward political form remained until 1991. In fact, many of Gorbachev's reforms were attempts to restore democracy to the soviet system.

The other main political continuity from 1917 to 1991 was the uninterrupted existence and rule of the Russian Communist Party (as the Bolshevik Party was renamed in 1918). Despite power struggles and purges, this party stayed in power for 74 years – though many claimed that the Communist Party of the Soviet Union eventually became very different from the original 1917 version. At the same time, the possibility of any political restoration of the old regime disappeared, with the execution of the Romanovs, and the closing down of all the main pre-1917 political parties.

Economy

Revolutionary victory in the economic sphere can be seen as even more pronounced than in the political sphere. Almost immediately after the Revolution, all the major economic assets of landowners and industrialists were taken over by peasants and workers. Later, first industry and then the land were nationalised and declared to be the inalienable property of the people. Though Soviet leaders never claimed to have established communism, these economic advances enabled them to argue that the Soviet Union had passed from the limited state capitalism of the New Economic Policy to the construction of a socialist society.

Despite the privileges of the bureaucratic elites who came to dominate the Soviet Union from the 1930s onwards, private ownership of major economic assets was never restored until after the collapse of the USSR in 1991.

In addition, one of the aims of the revolutionaries of 1917 had been to modernise and expand the Russian economy, and under Stalin the Soviet Union rapidly became a major industrial nation, although the process involved much hardship. One consequence of this extensive economic development was that a restoration of pre-1917 capitalism was rendered impossible, in that the assets which had been nationalised soon became only a very minute percentage of the Soviet Union's total industrial enterprises.

This industrial expansion also enabled the Soviet Union to withstand the Nazi onslaught of 1941–45, to achieve some notable firsts in space exploration and, for a time, to engage in an arms race with the world's wealthiest and most powerful superpower.

Society

Most of the major social gains which followed the 1917 Revolution were maintained and even improved and extended. There were notable achievements in education: vast resources were put into educating the mass of the population, with the result that by the 1970s the Soviet Union had a greater proportion of its population with higher education qualifications than any other country in the world.

Significant long-term improvements were also made in health and housing, despite several ups and downs resulting from invasion and other crises. Considerable strides were also taken towards women's emancipation. Although the early advances of 1917–29 were partially undermined under Stalin, women in the Soviet Union generally had more equality with men than did women in the more advanced capitalist states.

Defeat

However, as we have seen in relation to other revolutions, the story of any revolution is rarely one of total victory or total defeat. Certainly, many have claimed that the Russian Revolution was defeated, and that revolutionary continuity was broken, much earlier than 1991.

Some have attempted to argue that a form of capitalism – state capitalism – was restored under Stalin. Many more, with greater evidence, reject the argument that capitalism was restored but claim that the revolutionary continuity was only apparent. They see the external features of Soviet politics and economics as mere shells, concealing a very different set of realities, which often had little in common with the idealistic aspirations of 1917.

For instance, income inequalities between different sections of society were reintroduced after 1921, and greatly widened under Stalin and his successors. In addition, it was clear that from 1921 onwards the mass of the working classes were progressively deprived of active political power by the growing bureaucratic elite. Though the forms of soviet government continued, and trade unions were never abolished, these institutions were denied any opportunity for effective independent action.

Revolutionary defeat is seen much more starkly in the triumph of Stalin in the 1930s, which saw the removal, expulsion or execution of all the leading revolutionaries of 1917. Further, the idea of world revolution was progressively ignored by Stalin, who preferred to follow a much more conservative foreign policy designed primarily to secure the continued existence of the Soviet Union. For example, Comintern – set up by Lenin and Trotsky in 1919 to help spread world revolution – was increasingly controlled and manipulated by Moscow, and was finally closed down by Stalin in 1943.

Yet it is possible to see Stalinism as, at least in part, a form of revolutionary dictatorship which – although it debased or dismantled several aspects of early revolutionary socialist ideals and democracy – carried out, from above, a new phase of the social and economic revolutions begun in 1917. Thus the forced collectivisation of agriculture, the brutal aspects of the Five Year Plans and the show trials and purges can all be seen as rational – and revolutionary – responses to the extremely unfavourable internal and external political, economic and cultural conditions faced by the Soviet state in the 1930s.

A news-sheet produced by Trotsky's supporters in New York in March 1938. Why is this such effective propaganda?

Significantly, Trotsky (Stalin's main opponent after the death of Lenin) did not see these events – including his own deportation in 1929 – as ending the revolution, though he did see both method and content as unintentionally increasing the risk of eventual counter-revolution. The actions of Stalin and his successors can thus be seen as an attempt to continue and extend the revolutionary gains of 1917 and thus as a victory, rather than a defeat, for revolution. Any restorationist tendencies they may have unleashed took another 60 years to gain the upper hand.

This would explain the endurance of the political institutions and ideology of Bolshevism, as it is difficult to imagine their continued survival without there being at least some revolutionary purpose and content remaining after 1917, or even after 1939.

Conclusion: the end of history?

As we have seen, after the apparent end of each revolution, conservatives and reactionaries have attempted to prevent the outbreak of future revolutions. In addition, in the immediate aftermath of successful restoration, moderates and conservatives alike have confidently predicted that the era of revolution was over. Yet such fervent hopes in 1815, 1849 and 1871 were premature, and were successively dashed, as new revolutionary outbreaks and waves continued to emerge. After 1945, and the establishment of semi-revolutionary regimes in eastern Europe, waves of revolution broke out in Third World countries such as Vietnam, Cuba and Angola, most notably between 1959 and 1962 and, especially, between 1974 and 1980.

Despite this, after the collapse of the Eastern European and Soviet regimes in the period 1989–91, commentators such as Francis Fukuyama have repeated such conservative optimism, speaking of the 'end of history'. In part, this is based on the argument that the ideals of the French Revolution of 1789 – liberty, equality and fraternity – have finally triumphed, thereby allowing an un-interrupted future of capitalist development.

Yet, as has been seen, as early as 1792 many people felt that equality and liberty meant *economic* equality and *social* liberty not just the narrow political aspects which satisfied the liberal middle classes. From the sans-culottes of 1792–95, and Babeuf's attempted egalitarian uprising of 1796, many revolutionaries have made it clear that they consider the slogans of 1789 to be largely unfulfilled, and therefore still valid for the world at large – and still to be fought for.

Consequently, given the continued existence of economic exploitation, mass poverty and social injustice after 1815, it is not surprising that Europe was to see many more revolutions. Despite the eventual defeat in 1991 of the Russian Revolution of 1917, it is important to remember that starvation, inequality and injustice are still global phenomena. Therefore revolutionaries and revolutions are likely to continue to erupt in the future, until human hopes for a better and fairer world have been achieved.

In particular, the collapse of the Soviet Union should not be seen as the extinction of Marxism as a powerful revolutionary force. In fact, the ultimate failure of the political deformation of Marxism known as Stalinism can be seen as final proof of its inadequacies, and a vindication of Trotsky's criticisms. The end of Stalinism may thus result in a return to, and a resurgence of, Marx's revolutionary but less dogmatic communist politics and ideology. For many, orthodox Marxism is simply a logical extension of the more radical socialist interpretation, first given by Babeuf, to the 1789 ideals of liberty, equality and fraternity.

The demand for the full implementation of these ideals, increasingly with a socialist or communist element, was much to the fore in all the main revolutionary upheavals after 1789. Significantly perhaps, two hundred years later, in 1989, they formed the core demands of the revolutionary crowds in the cities of Eastern Europe, and in Tiananmen Square, Beijing. Events in Eastern Europe since then suggest that mass disappointment is emerging as people discover that the new political liberty is being accompanied by the loss of the old, albeit limited, social and economic equality which had existed before 1989.

Connected now to growing concern about environmental degradation and destruction, and about the resurgence of racism, these ideals are likely to confront the new millennium with the same revolutionary challenges, as the hopes associated with them remain on the political agenda. Thus, for generations to come, progressives – and revolutions – are likely to continue to be inspired by the revolutionary demand for liberty, equality and fraternity, in all its social and economic, as well as its political, aspects.

Indeed, there are signs once again, after a political lull beginning in the mid-1970s, of a new wave of youth radicalisation and the emergence of new social movements, as well as a revival of the more traditional workers' movements. Furthermore, the core demands of such ecological, feminist and anti-racist movements, and their emancipatory project of a society free from exploitation and oppression, still remain those 1789 ideals of liberty, equality and fraternity.

Document case study

Soviet isolation and collapse, 1917–91

10.1 The difficulties caused by the failure of revolutions outside Russia

V. I. Lenin, 'Better Fewer, But Better', 2 March 1923

The general feature of our present life is the following: we have destroyed capitalist industry and have done our best to raze to the ground the medieval institutions and landed proprietorship . . . It is not easy for us, however, to keep going until the socialist revolution is victorious in more developed countries . . . Moreover, the international situation, too, threw Russia back and, by and large, reduced the labour productivity of the people to a level considerably below prewar. The West European capitalist powers, partly deliberately and partly unconsciously, did everything they could to throw us back, to utilize the elements of the civil war in Russia in order to spread as much ruin in the country as possible. It was precisely this way out of the imperialist war that seemed to

have many advantages. They argued somewhat as follows: 'If we fail to overthrow the revolutionary system in Russia, we shall, at all events, hinder its progress towards socialism.' And from their point of view they could argue in no other way. In the end, their problem was half solved. They failed to overthrow the new system created by the revolution, but they did prevent it from at once taking the step forward that would have justified the forecasts of the socialists, that would have enabled the latter to develop the productive forces with enormous speed, to develop all the potentialities which, taken together, would have produced socialism; socialists would thus have proved to all and sundry that socialism contains within itself gigantic forces and that mankind had now entered into a new stage of development of extraordinarily brilliant prospects . . . May we hope that the internal antagonisms and conflicts between the thriving imperialist countries of the East will give us a second respite as they did the first time, when the campaign of the West European counterrevolution in support of the Russian counterrevolution broke down owing to the antagonisms in the camp of the counterrevolutionaries of the West and the East, in the camp of the Eastern and Western exploiters, in the camp of Japan and the USA?
March 2, 1923.
Source: V. I. Lenin, *Selected works*, vol. 3, Moscow, 1975, pp. 723–24

10.2 The roots of bureaucratic degeneration in the Soviet state

L. Trotsky, writing about what he described as the 'Soviet Thermidor', 1937

It is sufficiently well known that every revolution up to this time has been followed by a reaction, or even a counter-revolution. This, to be sure, has never thrown the nation all the way back to its starting point, but it has always taken from the people the lion's share of their conquests. The victims of the first reactionary wave have been, as a general rule, those pioneers, initiators, and instigators who stood at the head of the masses in the period of the revolutionary offensive. In their stead people of the second line, in league with the former enemies of the revolution, have been advanced to the front . . .

This reaction has developed in a series of consecutive waves. External conditions and events have vied with each other in nourishing it. Intervention followed intervention. The revolution got no direct help from the west. Instead of the expected prosperity of the country an ominous destitution reigned for long. Moreover, the outstanding representatives of the working class either died in the civil war, or rose a few steps higher and broke away from the masses . . .

Before he felt out his own course, the bureaucracy felt out Stalin himself. He brought it all the necessary guarantees: the prestige of an old Bolshevik, a strong character, narrow vision, and close bonds with the political machine as the sole source of his influence. The success which fell upon him was a surprise at first to Stalin himself. It was the friendly welcome of the new ruling group, trying to free itself from the old principles and from the control of the masses, and having need of a reliable arbiter in its inner affairs. A secondary figure before the masses and in the events of the revolution, Stalin revealed himself as the indubitable leader of the Thermidorian bureaucracy, as first in its midst . . .

The bureaucracy conquered something more than the Left Opposition. It conquered the Bolshevik party. It defeated the program of Lenin, who had seen the chief danger in the conversion of the organs of the state 'from servants of society to lords over society'. It defeated all these enemies, the Opposition, the party and Lenin, not with ideas and arguments, but with its own social weight. The leaden rump of the bureaucracy outweighed the head of the revolution. That is the secret of the Soviet's Thermidor . . .

Source: L. Trotsky, *The revolution betrayed*, 5th edn, New York, 1972, pp. 88–94

10.3 Socialism in One Country and the Five Year Plans

Stalin on the need to build up what he called the 'socialist fatherland' through the Five Year Plans in February 1931. Stalin remained ruler of the Soviet Union until 1953

In the past we had no fatherland, nor could we have had one. But now that we have overthrown capitalism and power is in our hands, in the hands of the people, we have a fatherland, and we must uphold its independence. Do you want our socialist fatherland to be beaten and to lose its independence? If you do not want this, you must put an end to its backwardness in the shortest possible time and develop a Bolshevik tempo in building up its socialist economy . . .

To slacken the tempo would mean falling behind. And those who fall behind get beaten. But we do not want to be beaten. No, we refuse to be beaten! . . . We are fifty or a hundred years behind the advanced countries. We must make good this distance in ten years. Either we do it or we shall go under.

Source: S. Fitzgerald, *The Russian Revolution*, 2nd edn, Oxford, 1994, p. 130

10.4 The Soviet Constitution of 1977

The Constitution (Fundamental Law) of the USSR, 1977, introduced by Brezhnev, which remained the basis of Soviet politics until the reforms of Gorbachev after 1985

The Great October Socialist Revolution, made by the workers and peasants of Russia under the leadership of the Communist Party headed by Lenin, overthrew capitalist and landowner role, broke the fetters of oppression, established the dictatorship of the proletariat, and created the Soviet state, a new type of state, the basic instrument for defending the gains of the revolution and for building socialism and communism. Humanity thereby began the epoch-making turn from capitalism to socialism . . .

The strength of socialism was vividly demonstrated by the immortal feat of the Soviet people and their Armed Forces in achieving their historic victory in the Great Patriotic War (the Second World War). This victory consolidated the influence and international standing of the Soviet Union and created new opportunities for growth of the forces of socialism, national liberation, democracy and peace throughout the world.

Continuing their creative endeavours, the working people of the Soviet Union have ensured rapid all-round development of the country and steady improvement of the socialist system. The leading role of the Communist Party, the vanguard of all the people, has grown.

In the USSR a developed socialist society has been built. The Soviet people, guided by the ideas of scientific communism and true to their revolutionary traditions, relying on the great social, economic, and political gains of socialism, striving for further development of socialist democracy, taking into account the international position of the USSR as part of the world system of socialism, and conscious of their international responsibility, preserving continuity of the ideas and principles of the first Soviet Constitution of 1918, the 1924 Constitution of the USSR and the 1936 Constitution of the USSR, hereby affirm the principles of the social structure and policy of USSR, and define the rights, freedoms and obligations of citizens, and the principles of the organisation of the socialist state of the whole people, and its aims, and proclaim these in this Constitution.

Source: D. Lane, *State and politics in the USSR*, Oxford, 1985, pp. 346–47

10.5 Gorbachev and the revival of socialist democracy

(i) M. Gorbachev, Report to the 27th Congress of the CPSU, February 1986

Lenin wrote back in 1917 that Marx and Engels rightly ridiculed the 'mere memorising and repetition of formulas, that at best are capable only of marking out general tasks, which are necessarily modifiable by the concrete economic and political conditions of each particular period of the historical process'. Those are the words comrades, that every one of us must ponder and act upon . . .

In these days, many things, in fact everything, will depend upon how effectively we will succeed in using the advantages and possibilities of the socialist system . . . in bringing the out of date social patterns and methods of work abreast of the changing conditions.

(ii) M. Gorbachev, Address to 18th Congress of Soviet Trade Unions, April 1987

We possess necessary political experience and theoretical potential to resolve the task facing society. One thing is clear: we should advance without fail along the path of reorganisation. If the reorganisation peters out the consequences will be far more serious for society as a whole and for every Soviet person in particular . . . I will put it bluntly: those who have doubts about the expediency of further democratisation apparently suffer from one serious drawback which is of great political significance and meaning – they do not believe in our people. They claim that democracy will be used by our people to disorganise society and undermine discipline, to undermine the strength of the system. I think we cannot agree to that. Democracy is not the opposite of order. It is the order of a greater degree, based not on implicit obedience, mindless execution of instructions, but on fully-fledged, active participation by all the community in all society's affairs . . . Democracy means self-control by society, confidence in civic maturity and awareness of social duty in Soviet people. Democracy is unity of right and duties. The deepening of democracy is certainly no easy matter. And there is no need to fear should everything not proceed smoothly at once, should there be potholes if not gullies . . . The more democracy we have, the faster we shall advance along the road to reorganisation and social renewal, and the more order and discipline we shall have in our social home. So it is either democracy or social inertia and conservatism. There is no third way, comrades.

Source: T. Ali, *Revolution from above: where is the Soviet Union going?*, London, 1988, pp. 4–5, 11–12

10.6 Possible outcomes of Gorbachev's reforms

Ernest Mandel, a Belgian economist and political theorist, was a leading member of the official Trotskyist Fourth International

Revolutions, however, in spite of the wishes of Gorbachev and the Social Democrats, are the product of exacerbated social and political contradictions and are not created by hidden conspirators. There will still be revolutions, even if they are not supported from Moscow. Marxism explains why these revolutions occur. It also explains the contradictions in Soviet society which gave rise to Gorbachev. It offers a coherent account of the whole crisis of our epoch and is capable of inspiring workers and youth. Where is the Soviet Union headed under Gorbachev? . . .

Another possibility is that Gorbachev will be outflanked by the radicalization of a section of leading cadres in the party which combines with a mass anti-bureaucratic mobilization. This will lead to a 'Moscow spring'. In this case, the conservative wing of the bureaucracy would prefer Gorbachev as a lesser evil rather than risk a real revolution from below. Whether or not this happens depends on the scale of the mobilization in the next two or three years and on the degree of radicalization that takes place inside the party. We think that this is not a likely outcome.

The third scenario is a more pessimistic one: the failure of the Gorbachev reform. If a mass mobilization does not develop, largely as a result of deteriorating conditions of life and work; if perestroika is an economic failure; if the conservative faction of the *nomenklatura* decide that glasnost is too risky; then the democratization process could be brought to a halt. But it would be difficult, if not impossible, to return to the status quo. Too much has already happened: social forces have been awakened; freedom of criticism has gone too far. There could not be a 'normalization' of the kind we saw in Czechoslovakia.

The fourth variant remains. Delays in the improvement of living and working conditions will transform working-class scepticism into virulent discontent and eventually mass action. The masses will seize the opportunities offered by glasnost to begin a vast movement of self-organization which becomes more and more centralized. The slogan 'All Power to the Soviets' will be revived in its classic form and meaning, and in socio-economic conditions much more favourable than existed in 1917, 1923 or 1927. A new political leadership will emerge from the working class and from the socialist intelligentsia which will help the masses in the achievement of their fundamental objectives. The political revolution, in the classical Marxist sense of the term, will triumph . . .

The conclusion which follows is that Soviet society has begun to move and no one can bring this movement to a halt. Stalinism and Brezhnevism are definitely at an end. The Soviet people, the international proletariat, the whole of humanity can breathe a great sigh of relief. The world is no longer as it used to be.

Source: E. Mandel, *Beyond Perestroika: the future of Gorbachev's USSR*, London, 1989, pp. xv–xvi

10.7 The collapse of the Soviet Union, 1991

The dramatic changes that have taken place in what used to be the Soviet Union have been at the centre of international attention since they were launched in the mid 1980s. It was certainly a change from the grey uniformity of the later Brezhnev years. The Soviet Union was suddenly under the control of a youthful and imaginative General Secretary with a personable wife by his side. The official ideology came under vigorous assault and a doctrine of 'socialist pluralism' was promoted in its place. Competitive elections were held to the first working parliament in Soviet history. The media began to reflect a variety of points of view . . .

The impact of all these changes, by the early 1990s, was still somewhat unclear. Democratisation, for instance, has led to an uneasy combination of party control and democratic accountability, and then, after the end of the communist rule in late 1991, to a form of parliamentary government that was difficult to reconcile with a powerful presidency . . .

There was some surprise that the Soviet leader continued to defend the Communist Party, whose role in the attempted coup had been obscure. Later, however, when the complicity of the party leadership became clear, Gorbachev resigned the general secretaryship and called upon the Central Committee to take the 'difficult but honourable decision to dissolve itself' . . .

The Soviet Union itself was a still greater casualty of the coup. Launched to block the signature of a new union treaty, the conspirators – in the end – accelerated the collapse of the state they had sought to preserve . . .

The post-Soviet era had begun.

Source: S. White, *After Gorbachev*, 4th edn, Cambridge, 1993, pp. ix, 26–27

Document case-study questions

1 What, according to Document 10.2, was the nature of the relationship between Stalin and the bureaucratic caste, in the process described by Trotsky as 'the Soviet Thermidor'?

2 From what you have read in this book and elsewhere, explain *briefly* the following references: (a) The West European capitalist powers (Document 10.1), (b) the Russian counter-revolution (Document 10.1), (c) the Central Committee (Document 10.7).

3 How useful are Documents 10.3 and 10.4 as historical evidence of Stalin's commitment to the revolutionary socialist ideals of 1917?

4 Assess the reliability of Documents 10.5 and 10.6 as evidence of the motives behind Gorbachev's reforms from 1985 to 1991.

5 How far do these *seven* documents, and any other evidence known to you, support the view that the socialist development of the Soviet Union ended with Stalin's rise to power in the 1930s?

Select bibliography

General

There are many good texts which deal either with revolutions specifically or with the general history of Europe during the period covered in this book. For revolutions, J. Dunn, *Modern revolutions: an introduction to the analysis of a political phenomenon*, Cambridge, 1989, is very interesting though rather difficult. For the overall history of Europe, F. L. Ford, *Europe, 1780–1830*, 2nd edn, London, 1989, is very sound, while E. J. Hobsbawm, *The age of revolution: Europe 1789–1848*, London, 1973, and *The age of capital: 1848–1875*, London, 1977, offer a stimulating overview.

Also useful are: M. S. Anderson, *The ascendancy of Europe*, 2nd edn, London, 1985; H. Arendt, *On revolution*, New York, 1965; and P. Calvert, *Revolution*, London, 1970.

The French Revolution, 1789

There are very many texts that deal with the history of the French Revolution. For a relatively short overview, see either D. Townson, *France in revolution*, London, 1990, or D. G. Wright, *Revolution and terror in France 1789–1795*, 2nd edn, London, 1990. Also extremely useful is D. M. G. Sutherland, *France, 1789–1815: revolution and counter-revolution*, London, 1985. See also: W. Doyle, *The origins of the French Revolution*, Oxford, 1980; N. Hampson, *The French Revolution: a concise history*, London, 1975; G. Rudé, *The French Revolution*, London, 1989; and J. H. Shennan, *France before the Revolution*, London, 1983.

For ideology, parties and leaders, see N. Hampson, *The Enlightenment*, London, 1968; N. Hampson, *The French Revolution and democracy*, Reading, 1983; G. Rudé, *Robespierre*, London, 1975; and R. B. Rose, *The Enragés: socialists of the French Revolution?*, Melbourne, 1965.

For women, see L. Kelly, *Women of the French Revolution*, London, 1987; and O. Hufton, 'Women in revolution, 1780–96', *Past and Present*, vol. 53, 1971.

The 1848 revolutions

For a good overall view of the 1848 revolutions, see P. Jones, *The 1848 revolutions*, 2nd edn, London, 1991. An up-to-date and fuller treatment will be found in J. Sperber, *The European revolutions, 1848–1851*, Cambridge, 1994. Also useful are: R. Price, *The revolutions of 1848*, London, 1988; and P. N. Stearns, *The revolutions of 1848*, London, 1974.

For France, see M. Agulhon, *The republican experiment 1848–52*, Cambridge, 1983; and T. Zeldin, *France 1848–1945*, Oxford, 1979.

For the Habsburg Empire, see D. Ward, *1848: The fall of Metternich*, London, 1970; and C. A. Macartney, *The Habsburg Empire, 1790–1918*, London, 1969.

For the German states, see F. Eyck (ed.), *The revolutions of 1848–49*, Edinburgh, 1972; and W. Carr, *A history of Germany, 1815–1985*, London, 1985.

For the Italian states, see H. Hearder, *Italy in the age of the Risorgimento*, London, 1983; and D. Mack Smith, *The making of Italy, 1796–1866*, London, 1988.

For a discussion of social history aspects, see P. Robertson, *Revolutions of 1848: a social history*, New York, 1965.

The Paris Commune, 1871

There is a wide range of texts on the Paris Commune, several of which offer a particular slant. A sound survey is provided by S. Edwards, *The Paris Commune, 1871*, London, 1971; while R. Thombs, *The war against Paris, 1871*, Cambridge, 1981, gives a more recent account. Also useful are: A. Horne, *The fall of Paris: the siege and Commune, 1870–71*, London, 1965; E. Schulkind, *The Paris Commune of 1871 – the view from the left*, London, 1972; and R. L. Williams, *The French Revolution of 1870–1871*, London, 1969.

For the role of women, see E. Thomas, *The women incendiaries*, London, 1967.

The Russian Revolution, 1917

There are a great many texts available on the Russian Revolution. Straightforward and up-to-date accounts are provided by S. Fitzpatrick, *The Russian Revolution*, 2nd edn, Oxford, 1994; M. McCauley, *The Soviet Union since 1917*, London, 1981; and A. Wood, *The Russian Revolution*, 2nd edn, London, 1986. Though written over thirty years ago, E. H. Carr, *The Bolshevik revolution, 1917–23*, 3 vols., London, 1966, provides a very sound and detailed coverage. Also useful are: G. Hosking, *A history of the Soviet Union, 1917–1991*, London, 1992; D. Lane, *State and politics in the USSR*, Oxford, 1985; and R. Pipes, *The Russian Revolution*, vols. 1 and 2, London, 1990.

For ideology, parties and leaders, see I. Deutscher, *The prophet armed, Trotsky 1879–1921*, Oxford, 1954; and A. B. Ulam, *Lenin and the Bolsheviks*, London, 1996.

For the role of women, see B. E. Clements, *Bolshevik women*, Cambridge, 1997; C. Porter, *Alexandra Kollontai*, London, 1980; and R. H. McNeal, *Bride of the revolution*, Michigan, 1972.

Chronologies

The French Revolution

1787   *May–July:* Suspension of the *parlements*; Revolt of the Aristocracy
      Aug–Sep: Brienne replaced by Necker; *parlements* recalled

1789   *Apr:* Riots in Paris and the provinces
      5 May: Meeting of the Estates-General
      20 June: Tennis Court Oath
      11–14 July: Dismissal of Necker; fall of the Bastille
      4 Aug: Abolition of feudal rights; Declaration of Rights
      5 Oct: March of the Women to Versailles
      2 Nov: Decrees on the Church and local government

1790   *Feb–Mar:* Religious conflict in Nîmes
      June: Abolition of the nobility
      July: Civil Constitution of the Clergy
      Nov: Enforcement of the clerical oath, accepted by Louis XVI

1791   *June:* Flight to Varennes
      July: Massacre on the Champ de Mars
      Sep: King accepts the Constitution of 1791; Constituent Assembly dissolved
      Nov–Dec: King vetoes decrees against *émigrés* and clergy

1792   *Mar:* Brissotin Ministry
      Apr: Declaration of war with Austria
      June: First invasion of the Tuileries
      July: Brunswick Manifesto (published in Paris 3 August) and agitation in the Paris *sections*
      Aug: Revolution of 10 August; insurrectionary Commune set up; king suspended; beginning of the First Terror
      Sep: Fall of Verdun; September Massacres; Battle of Valmy; meeting of the Convention; abolition of the monarchy; republic declared
      Dec: Trial of the king

1793   *Jan:* Execution of the king
      Feb: War with Britain and Holland; food riots in Paris; the *Enragés* agitations
      Mar: War with Spain; outbreak of revolt in the Vendée
      Apr: Establishment of the Committee of Public Safety; first Maximum (grain)
      May: Federalist revolts at Lyons, Marseilles, Caen and Bordeaux
      June: Fall of the Girondins; Jacobin Constitution of 1793

1793   *July:* Robespierre entered the Committee of Public Safety; Revolutionary Tribunal reorganised; assassination of Marat

Aug: Levée en masse (conscription); surrender of Toulon to the British

Sep: Beginning of Year II of the Republic; Terror officially established; creation of the Parisian *armée révolutionnaire*; Law of Suspects; Law of General Maximum

Oct: Government declared 'revolutionary until the peace'; recapture of Lyons by republican forces; trial and execution of the Girondins

Nov: Revolutionary calendar adopted

Dec: Reorganisation of revolutionary government by the Law of 14 Frimaire; defeat of the Vendée rebels

1794   *Feb:* Laws of Ventôse (to confiscate property of suspects, and to give proceeds to the poor)

Mar–Apr: Arrest and execution of the Hébertists and Dantonists

May: Attempts to assassinate Robespierre

June: Law of 22 Prairial

July: Maximum wage legislation; arrest and execution of Robespierre and his followers

Nov: Jacobin Club closed

Dec: Abolition of the Law of General Maximum

1795   *Apr:* Rising of Germinal

May: Rising of Prairial

Aug: Constitution of the Year III; Law of the Two-Thirds

Oct: Rising of Vendémiaire; dissolution of the Convention and the beginning of the Directory

The 1848 revolutions

		France	Habsburg Empire
1848	Jan		
	Feb	24th Abdication of Louis Philippe 25th First Proclamation of the provisional government 26th Proclamation of the Second Republic 27th Establishment of National Workshops Scheme	
	Mar	7th Lamartine's Manifesto to Europe 23rd Constituent Assembly elected	13th Resignation of Metternich 14th–15th Formulation of the demands of the Hungarians
	Apr		11th Ferdinand I approves the April Laws
	May		15th Second uprising in Vienna 17th Habsburg Imperial Court leaves Vienna for Innsbruck
	June	23rd–26th June Days uprising in Paris	2nd Pan-Slav Congress meets in Vienna 16th Windischgrätz bombards Prague 28th Pan-Slav Congress ruthlessly suppressed by Windischgrätz
	July		22nd Constituent Assembly meets in Vienna
	Sep		11th Jellačic begins invasion of Hungary
	Oct		6th October Days uprising in Vienna 31st Windischgrätz crushes Vienna revolution
	Nov		21st Schwarzenberg becomes chancellor
	Dec	10th Louis Napoleon elected president of Second Republic	2nd Ferdinand abdicates in favour of Franz-Josef
1849	Feb		
	Mar		4th Stadion Constitution declared 7th Schwarzenberg dissolves Kremsier Reichstag (Constituent Assembly)
	Apr		
	July		
	Aug		13th Hungarians defeated at Vilagos, and finally surrender

German states	Italian states		
	12th Revolution in Palermo, Sicily	Jan	1848
		Feb	
5th Heidelberg Liberals call for a Vorparlament 14th–15th Violence breaks out in Berlin, Prussia 18th Frederick William IV of Prussia promises reform	23rd Piedmont declares war against the Habsburgs	Mar	
10th Prussian troops enter Schleswig-Holstein		Apr	
18th Meeting of the Frankfurt Assembly		May	
		June	
	23rd Radetzky defeats Piedmont at Custozza; Milan re-occupied	July	
		Sep	
		Oct	
	24th Pope leaves Rome	Nov	
		Dec	
	9th Mazzini proclaims Roman Republic	Feb	1849
	23rd Final defeat of Italians at Novara	Mar	
3rd Frederick William IV rejects Frankfurt Assembly's offer of crown of a united Germany		Apr	
	3rd French troops occupy Rome after suppressing Roman Republic	July	
	23rd Venice finally surrenders	Aug	

The Paris Commune

1870 *4 Sep:* News of defeat and surrender of emperor at Sedan reaches Paris; Third Republic proclaimed

     18 Sep: Siege of Paris by Prussians begins

     31 Oct: Riots in Paris after surrender at Metz

1871 *5 Jan:* Prussians begin bombardment of Paris

     28 Jan: Siege of Paris ends, after signing of armistice

     8 Feb: Elections for new National Assembly

     15 Feb: Pay for National Guard cancelled

     17 Feb: Thiers elected leader of new government

     26–28 Feb: Rebel National Guards seize 200 cannons

     15 Mar: Central committee of National Guard elected

     18 Mar: Government attempt to recapture cannons at Montmartre sparks off uprising; government flees to Versailles

     22 Mar: Suppression begins of *communes* in Lyons, Toulouse, Saint-Etienne, Narbonne and Marseilles

     26 Mar: Elections held for Commune in Paris

     28 Mar: New Commune takes power

     30 Mar: Start of civil war between Paris Commune and Versailles government

     4 Apr: Archbishop of Paris arrested as hostage after *communard* prisoners shot on battlefield

     11 Apr: Formation of the Women's Union for the Defence of Paris and Aid to the Wounded

     19 Apr: Commune issues Declaration, outlining aims and programme

     1 May: Committee of Public Safety formed; Versailles begins bombardment of Paris

     9 May: Fort d'Issy captured by Versailles troops; Delescluze made Delegate for War

     21 May: Final full session of the Commune; Versailles troops enter Paris

     25 May: Last meeting of Commune; Delescluze dies on barricades

     26 May: Commune executes hostages

     27 May: Mass executions of *communards* begin at Père-Lachaise cemetery

     28 May: Last barricade captured; Commune ends

     Nov: First death sentences for *communards* after trials

The Russian Revolution

See footnote on p. 28.

1917 *3 Mar:* Strike begins at Putilov factories

8 Mar: International Women's Day and workers' demonstrations; start of February Revolution

10 Mar: General strike

12 Mar: Unofficial meeting of Duma Committee; first meeting of Petrograd Soviet

14 Mar: Soviet Order Number 1 established

15 Mar: Provisional government formed from Duma Committee, Nicholas signs Decree of Abdication

16 Mar: New government publicly declared

27 Mar: Soviet issues an 'Address to the People of the Whole World'

16 Apr: Lenin returns to Petrograd

17 Apr: Lenin issues 'April Theses'

16–19 July: July Days uprising; Bolsheviks outlawed

19 July: Lenin flees from Petrograd

21 July: Kerensky becomes prime minister

31 July: Kornilov becomes commander-in-chief

8–14 Sep: Kornilov's attempted coup

8 Oct: Bolsheviks gain a majority in Petrograd Soviet; Trotsky elected as chairman

23 Oct: Bolshevik central committee commits itself to armed insurrection; Zinoviev and Kamenev opposed

25 Oct: Petrograd Soviet sets up Military Revolutionary Committee; Trotsky is chairman

5 Nov: Kerensky orders closing down of *Pravda* and *Izvestiya*; Lenin instructs the Bolsheviks to begin the rising against Kerensky's government

6 Nov: First session of the Congress of Soviets

6–7 Nov: Bolsheviks take control of Petrograd

7–8 Nov: Kerensky leaves Petrograd, hoping to rally support, but fails; Bolsheviks take the Winter Palace

9 Nov: Lenin informs the Congress of Soviets that the Bolshevik-led Petrograd Soviet has seized power in their name; Lenin becomes chairman of Sovnarkom (the new Soviet government)

21 Nov: Bolsheviks issue the Decrees on Land, on Peace, and on Workers' Control

24 Nov: Elections for Constituent Assembly begin

1918 *18–19 Jan:* Meeting and dissolution of the Constituent Assembly

28 Jan: Decree establishing the Red Army

3 Mar: Treaty of Brest-Litovsk

12 Mar: Soviet capital transferred to Moscow; Bolshevik Party renamed the Communist Party

4 Apr: Beginning of foreign interventions

May: Czech Legion begins to create problems for the Bolsheviks, which marks the start of the Civil War, between Reds and Whites

June: Decree on Nationalisation

July: Beginning of forced grain requisitions from the peasants

4 July: Russian state becomes the Russian Socialist Federal Soviet Republic

1918 *16–17 July:* Murder of Tsar and family at Ekaterinburg

5 Sep: Red Terror officially introduced, under control of Cheka

1919 *Mar:* First Congress of the Comintern

1920 *Mar:* Pilsudski launches Polish invasion of Russia

Apr: Red Army marches into Poland, but is forced back

Nov: The Civil War effectively ends with the defeat of the Whites in the Crimea

1921 Mar: Kronstadt Rising

Mar: Lenin introduces the NEP at the 10th Congress of the CPSU, which also accepts the decree against factionalism; other parties to be banned temporarily

1922–23 Lenin suffers a number of increasingly severe strokes that limit his ability to control events

1922 *Dec:* Soviet state becomes the USSR; Lenin completes his 'Testament', critical of all the leading Bolsheviks, then recommends dismissal of Stalin

1924 *21 Jan:* Lenin's death; struggle for power between the Triumvirs and Trotsky begins in earnest

Index

agriculture, in pre-revolutionary France, 18–19
Alexander II, Tsar of Russia, 16, 40
All-Russian Congress of Soviets, 30, 55, 118
American War of Independence, 22, 33
Anneke, Mathilde Franziska, 88
Austria: communist rising (1919), 78, 79; *see also* Habsburg Empire
Axelrod, Paul, 40, 41

Babeuf, François (Gracchus), 50, 113, 121, 122
Bakunin, Mikhail, 39
Balabanoff, Angelica, 92
Banquet Campaign (1846–48), 24, 35, 50
Bavaria: 1848 revolution in, 25–6, 63; impact of Russian Revolution (1917) on, 78, 79
Bismarck, Otto von, 27
Blanc, Louis, 51, 85
Blanqui, Auguste, 27, 36, 38, 39, 42, 43
Blanquism, and Paris Commune (1871), 38–9, 43, 53
Bochkareva, Maria L., 91
Bolsheviks, 29, 30, 41, 54–7, 65–8, 77–8; and counter-revolution in Russia, 108–10; and revolutionary continuity, 118; women activists, 90–1; *see also* Russian Revolution (1917)
Born, Stefan 51
bourgeoisie, *see* middle classes
Brest-Litovsk, Treaty of, 55, 78, 92, 108
Breteuil, Louis Auguste de, 59, 100
Brienne, Loménie de, 21
Brissot, Jacques Pierre, 33, 47
Britain, impact of Russian Revolution (1917) on, 78–9
Bukharin, Nikolai, 54, 55, 110
Burke, Edmund, 32, 73

Calonne, Charles-Alexandre de, 21
Carlsbad Decrees (1819), 34
Cattaneo, Carlo, 70
Champs de Mars massacre, 46, 60
Cheka (Russian Revolution (1917)), 4, 66, 68, 109
China, 34, 79, 122
civil war, 2; in Russia (1918–20), 4, 66, 67, 79, 108–9
class, and Russian Revolution (1917), 15
clergy, and French Revolution (1789), 8
Cluseret, Gustave, 39
Comintern, 79, 120

communism, 31, 39; and counter-revolution in Russia, 110
Communist Manifesto (1848), 77
Cordeliers Club, 47, 49, 82, 83
corvée, 18
counter-revolutions, 2, 5, 99–110; creeping, 99; and 1848 revolutions, 103–6; and French Revolution (1789), 100–3; international assistance for, 100; and Paris Commune (1871), 106–7; and Russian Revolution (1917), 108–10; violence and, 2, 4, 58, 99
coups, 1, 2, 3
Courbois, Joséphine, 87, 90
Couthon, Georges, 47
crisis of legitimacy, 20–1
crowds, 45; and 1848 revolutions, 51–2; and French Revolution (1789), 48–50; and Russian Revolution (1917), 55–7
Czechoslovakia, 1848 revolution in, 36–7, 104

d'Aelders, Etta Palm, 84, 94
Danton, Georges, 47, 61
Declaration of the Rights of Man and of the Citizen, 33, 82, 100
Declaration of the Rights of Women, 84, 93–4
democracy: as an international movement, 71; and 1848 revolutions, 34; and French Revolution (1789), 32; Gorbachev on, 125; and Russian Revolution (1917), 118
Déroin, Jeanne, 87
Dmitrieff, Elizabeth, 89

Eastern Europe, 58, 121, 122
economic developments, 3, 7–19, 31; and 1848 revolutions, 12–13; and French Revolution (1789), 9–11, 113; and Paris Commune (1871), 14; and Russian Revolution (1917), 16–17, 119
1848 revolutions, 5, 68–70; continuity, victory and defeat in, 114–17; and counter-revolution, 103–6; economic and social factors as causes of, 11–13; and ideology, 34–8; international impact of, 74–5; parties and leaders, 50–2; and political crisis, 23–6; as political and social revolutions, 4; and revolutionary crowds, 51–2; violence and, 58, 61–3; women's involvement in, 85–8
Encyclopédie (Diderot and d'Alembert), 33
Engels, Friedrich, 23, 39
England, political clubs, 73

Enlightenment ideology, 32–4, 72
Enragés, 47, 83, 84, 95, 96, 102
Estates-General, 22, 33
evolution, revolution linked to, 3
Excoffon, Béatrix, 89

fascism, 110
Figner, Vera, 91
First International, and Paris Commune (1871), 27, 38, 39, 43, 44, 53, 76, 106
First World War, 71; and Russian Revolution (1917), 17, 28–9, 78, 90
food riots, 10, 13, 17, 81
France, 1848 revolution, 11, 13, 24–5, 26, 35–6, 50, 51, 62, 68–9, 75, 85; continuity, victory and defeat in, 114; and counter-revolution, 103–4; and women, 85, 86–7, 87–8
Franco-Prussian War (1870–71), 14–15, 27, 42–3, 76
Frankel, Leo, 39
Frederick William IV, King of Prussia, 26, 36, 63, 68, 75, 105, 115
French Revolution (1789): and capture of Tuileries, 48–9, 60; Committee of Public Safety, 60; continuity, victory and defeat in, 111–13; and counter-revolution, 100–3; economic and social factors as causes of, 7–11, 18–19; and fall of the Bastille, 48, 59, 71, 72, 100; ideology and, 32–4, 121, 122; international impact of, 71, 72–4, 77; *journées*, 48, 60; October Days (1789), 81–2, 84; parties and leaders, 46–7; and political crisis, 21–3; as a political and social revolution, 4; and revolutionary crowds, 48–50; second stage, 5; and September massacres, 48, 49, 60, 102; and Sugar Riots (1792), 82; and Terror, 47, 59–61, 73, 101; Thermidor, 49, 50, 82–3, 84, 102, 110, 112, 113; and three estates, 8, 9, 22; and violence, 4, 59–61; and wars in Europe, 46, 59–60, 73–4, 82, 101; women's involvement in, 48, 81–4
Fukuyama, Francis, 121

Garibaldi, Anita, 88
German states, 1848 revolution, 12, 25–6, 34, 36, 37, 50, 52, 63, 68; continuity, victory and defeat in, 115–16; and counter-revolution, 105; and women, 86, 87, 88
Germany, Spartacist Rising in (1919), 78, 79
Girondins, 21, 47, 48, 49, 60, 61, 83, 84, 101
Gorbachev, Mikhail, 54, 118, 125–7
Gouges, Olympe de, 84, 93
Gramont, Duc de, 27
Guchkov, Alexander, 29
Guizot, François, 24, 50, 62, 68

Habsburg Empire, 1848 revolution, 25, 36–7, 50, 52, 62–3, 68, 69, 74–5, 85–6; continuity, victory and defeat in, 115; and counter-revolution, 104–5; women's involvement in, 85–6, 87

Hébertism, 34, 35, 38, 43, 47, 49, 61, 102
Held, Alexander, 51, 87
Herzen, Alexander, 40
Hugo, Victor, 36, 43, 68, 103
Hungary: communist rising in (1919), 78, 79; 1848 revolution in, 25, 36–7, 62, 63, 86, 104–5

ideology, 31–44; and 1848 revolutions, 34–8; and French Revolution (1789), 32–4, 121, 122; and Paris Commune (1871), 38; and Russian Revolution (1917), 34, 39–41, 118
industrialisation: and 1848 revolutions, 11, 12, 13; and Paris Commune (1871), 14; and Russian Revolution (1917), 16, 119
International Working Men's Association, *see* First International
Ireland, impact of French Revolution (1789) in, 73
Italian states, 1848 revolution, 37–8, 51, 52, 63, 68, 69–70, 75; continuity, victory and defeat in, 116; and counter-revolution, 105–6; and women, 86, 87, 88
Italian states, and support for French Revolution (1789), 72, 73
Italy, 78, 110

Jacobins, 21, 34, 46–7, 72, 73; and counter-revolution, 102; and Paris Commune (1871), 38, 43, 53, 63; and women, 83
Jellačić, Count Joseph, 104

Kamenev, Lev, 54, 55, 110
Kaskova, Ekaterina, 91
Kerensky, Alexander, 29–30, 54, 65, 91, 108
Kollontai, Alexandra, 92
Kolowratz, Count Francis von, 25
Kornilov, General Lavr, 29, 108
Kronstadt Rising (1921), 57, 66–7, 109
Krupskaya, Nadezhda, 92

Lacombe, Claire, 84, 96
Lafayette, Marquis de, 22, 60, 101
land nationalisation, and Russian Revolution (1917), 56–7, 119
leaders, 5, 45–6; of 1848 revolutions, 50–1; of French Revolution (1789), 46–7; of Paris Commune (1871), 52–3; of Russian Revolution (1917), 54–5
Lenin (Vladimir Illyich Ulyanov), 29, 41, 54, 55, 65, 66, 78, 92, 120; 'Better Fewer, But Better', 122–3; and counter-revolution, 108, 109; death of, 110; and Paris Commune (1871), 77, 78; Trotsky on, 124
Leo, André, 89
Léon, Pauline, 84
liberalism: and 1848 revolutions, 23, 25, 26, 34, 35, 36, 37, 38, 51, 52, 74, 75; and French Revolution (1789), 39; and Habsburg Empire, 115; and Russian Revolution (1917), 39–40; and Second Empire in France, 26–7
Liebknecht, Karl, 78, 79

Louis XVI, King of France, 21, 22, 23, 33, 48, 59, 60, 82, 101
Louis Philippe, King of the French, 24, 35, 62, 68, 74, 103, 112
Ludwig I, King of Bavaria, 25–6
Luxemburg, Rosa, 78, 79

Manin, Daniel, 50, 63, 70, 88
Marx, Karl, 23, 31, 38, 39, 41, 71, 116; and Paris Commune (1871), 44, 76–7, 79
Marxism, 8, 39, 40–1, 53, 122
Mazzini, Giuseppe, 37, 50, 86, 105
Mensheviks, 29, 41, 54, 65
Méricourt, Théroigne de, 84
Metternich, Clemens von, 23, 25, 26, 37, 38, 62, 63, 68, 69, 72, 74–5, 116
Michel, Louise, 89
middle classes: and 1848 revolutions, 11, 24, 25, 26, 35, 36, 50, 51, 52; and French Revolution (1789), 8, 48, 50, 73, 83, 112–13; in German states, 115; and Paris Commune (1871), 53; and Russian Revolution (1917), 15, 39, 41
Mirabeau, Honoré Gabriel Riqueti, Comte de, 22, 33
monarchy, and French Revolution (1789), 111–12, 113
Montagnards, 47, 49, 82, 83, 84, 102
Montesquieu, C. de, 32, 33
Montez, Lola, 25–6

Napoleon I, Emperor of France, 71, 74, 102–3, 111–12, 113
Napoleon III, Emperor (Louis Napoleon), 14, 26–7, 87, 112, 114
Narodnik movement in Russia, 40, 90
National Guard: and 1848 revolution, 25, 62; and French Revolution (1789), 48, 60, 82, 100; and Paris Commune (1871), 15, 27–8, 42, 43, 53, 64, 88
nationalism: and 1848 revolutions, 23, 34, 35, 36, 37, 38; and French Revolution (1789), 32
Necker, Jacques, 21, 59, 100
Nicholas II, Tsar of Russia, 28
nobility: and 1848 revolutions, 11, 25; and French Revolution (1789), 8, 21–2, 112; in pre-revolutionary France, 18; and Russian Revolution (1917), 15

Ollivier, Emile, 27
Orléans, Duc d' (Philippe-Egalité), 22
Otto-Peters, Luise, 88

Paris Commune (1871): communards' determination to resist, 42; continuity, victory and defeat in, 117–18; and counter-revolution, 106–7; economic and social factors as a cause of, 13–15; ideology and, 38–9; international impact of, 76–7, 79; Marx on operation of, 44; and opposition to Thiers' peace with Prussia, 42–3; parties and leaders, 52–3; political clubs and activitists in, 42, 43, 53; and political crisis, 26–8; and revolutionary crowds, 53; as a social revolution, 4; violence and, 63–4, 106–7; women's involvement in, 88–90
parties, see political parties
peasants: and 1848 revolutions, 11, 13; and French Revolution (1789), 9, 10, 18, 112–13; and Russian Revolution (1917), 15, 16, 17, 40
philosophes, see Enlightenment ideology
Pius IX, Pope, 37–8
Plekhanov, Georgi, 40, 41
political activists: in Paris Commune (1871), 42, 43, 52–3, 89–90; women, 84, 87–8, 89–90, 91–3
political clubs: and 1848 revolutions, 51, 86–7; and French Revolution (1789), 46–7, 48, 72, 73, 83–4, 101; and Paris Commune (1871), 42, 43, 53; and women, 83–4, 86–7, 89, 95–8
political crises, 20–30, 31, 45; and 1848 revolutions, 23–6; factors contributing to, 20–1; and French Revolution (1789), 21–3; and Paris Commune (1871), 26–8; and Russian Revolution (1917), 28–30
political parties, 32, 45–6; and French Revolution (1789), 46–7; and Russian Revolution (1917), 54–5
political revolution, 4
population, 9, 12, 16
populism, and Russian Revolution (1917), 40
poverty, 2, 3, 19
Proudhon, Pierre Joseph, 36, 39, 43, 87
Prussia: 1848 revolution in, 26, 36, 63, 115–16; see also Franco-Prussian War
putsch, 1

Radetzky, Count Joseph, 63, 69, 70, 105, 106
radicalism, and 1848 revolutions, 23
Rasputin, Gregori, 28
reforms, 2, 20
revolts/rebellions, 2
revolution: defining, 1, 2–3; stages of, 5; types of, 3–4
Robespierre, Maximilien, 34, 43, 47, 49–50, 58, 59, 61, 73, 83; and counter-revolution, 101, 102
Roland, Marie-Jeanne 'Manon', 84
Rousseau, Jean-Jacques, 32, 33, 34, 48, 84
Roux, Jacques, 47, 95
Rudé, George, 31
Russian Revolution (1917), 5, 15–17; and Civil War (1918–20), 4, 66, 67, 79, 108–9; continuity, victory and defeat in, 118–21; and counter-revolution, 108–10; and economic developments, 3, 16–17, 119; and failure of revolutions outside Russia, 122–3; ideology and, 34, 39–41, 118; international impact of, 77–9; July Days, 29, 65, 108; and Kronstadt Rising (1921), 57, 66–7, 109; and land and factory nationalisation, 56–7, 119;

Russian Revolution (1917) *cont.* March Revolution, 29, 65, 90, 118; and New Economic Policy, 55, 56, 109, 119; November Revolution, 29–30, 65–7, 90–1; parties and leaders, 54–5; Petrograd Soviet, 29; and political crisis, 28–30; and population, 16; and provisional government, 28–30, 65–6, 91; Rabotnitsa group, 91, 92; and revolutionary crowds, 55–7; as a social revolution, 4; and society, 15–16, 119; violence and, 64–8; and War Communism, 55, 56, 57, 109; women's involvement in, 28, 90–3

Saint-Just, Louis Antoine, 34, 47, 59
Saint-Simon, Claude, 36
Sand, George, 87
sans-culottes, 10, 43, 47, 48, 49, 50, 83, 113, 121; women, 84
Second World War, 71
Sidoli, Giuditta, 86, 88
Sieyès, Emmanuel Joseph, Abbé, 22, 33
social developments: and French Revolution (1789), 8, 112–13; and ideology, 31; and Russian Revolution (1917), 15–16, 119; *see also* economic developments
Social Revolutionaries (SRs) in Russia, 29, 40, 41, 54, 55, 57, 65, 66; women's involvement in, 90, 91–2
social revolutions, 4
socialism: as an international movement, 71; and 1848 revolutions, 34, 35, 38, 116–17; and French Revolution (1789), 32; and Paris Commune (1871), 38–9; and Russian Revolution (1917), 40; utopian, 38, 39; *see also* Marxism
Soviet Union: collapse of (1991), 3, 118, 119, 122; constitution of 1977, 124–5
Spain, 75, 78, 117
Spartacists, 78, 79
Spiridonova, Maria, 91–2
SRRW (Society of Revolutionary Republican Women), 83–4, 95–8
Stalin, Joseph, 54, 91, 110, 119
Stalinism, 110, 119–21, 122, 123–4
Stasova, Elena, 92
Stolypin, Peter, 16
strikes, and Russian Revolution (1917), 17, 78
students: and 1848 revolutions, 11, 35, 36, 37, 62, 63, 70; and Paris Commune (1871), 77; and Russian Revolution (1917), 16, 40

Switzerland, political clubs, 73

technological developments: and 1848 revolutions, 36; and international impact of revolutions, 71
Tennis Court Oath, 22
terror, 58–9; counter-revolutionary, 58, 99; and French Revolution (1789), 47, 59–61, 101; and Russian Revolution (1917), 66, 109
Thiers, Adolphe, 15, 24, 27, 42, 43, 50, 53, 64, 107, 117
Third International, *see* Comintern
Tocqueville, Alexis de, 32, 34
Trotsky, Leon, 5, 41, 54, 55, 66, 78, 109; and Stalin, 121, 122, 123–4
Turgot, Anne-Robert-Jacques, 18, 23

universal male suffrage, in France, 114, 117
universities, and 1848 revolutions, 35, 36

Varennes, flight to, 46, 60
Vergniaud, Pierre, 47
Vienna Settlement / Congress System (1815), 23, 112, 116
violence, 3–4, 58–70; and counter-revolution, 2, 4, 58, 99; and 1848 revolutions, 61–3; and French Revolution (1789), 8, 59–61; and Paris Commune (1871), 63–4, 106–7; and Russian Revolution (1917), 64–8
Voltaire, F., 32

Witte, Sergei, 16, 41
women's involvement in revolutions, 3, 80–98; 1848 revolutions, 85–8; French Revolution (1789), 48, 81–4; Paris Commune (1871), 88–90; Russian Revolution (1917), 28, 90–3
working classes: and 1848 revolutions, 50–1, 52, 116–17; and French Revolution (1789), 43, 47, 48, 49, 50, 83, 84, 113; and Gorbachev's reforms, 126; and Paris Commune (1871), 44, 53; and political clubs, 73; and Russian Revolution (1917), 16–17, 40–1, 120; women 80

Young, Arthur, 18–19, 32
Young Italy, 37
young people, 2–3; *see also* students

Zasulich, Vera, 90, 92
Zinoviev, Grigori, 54, 55, 92, 110